A Political Economy of the Measurement of Inflation

Florence Jany-Catrice

A Political Economy of the Measurement of Inflation

The case of France

palgrave
macmillan

Florence Jany-Catrice
Faculty of Economics and Social Sciences
University of Lille
Lille, France

Member of the IAS-Princeton (2020–2021)
Princeton, NJ, USA

ISBN 978-3-030-59939-3 ISBN 978-3-030-59940-9 (eBook)
https://doi.org/10.1007/978-3-030-59940-9

This Palgrave Macmillan imprint is published by the registered company Springer Nature Switzerland AG.
The registered company address is: Gewerbestrasse 11, 6330 Cham, Switzerland

Contents

List of Figures

List of Tables

List of Boxes

Introduction[1]

Inflation fell spectacularly in France in the second half of the 1980s. Between 1980 and 1985 it was running at an average of 9.6%; between 1985 and 1990, the annual average rate fell to 3.1%. And yet the economist Jean-Paul Piriou, in his book *L'indice des prix*, first published in 1983 and reprinted in 1992, describes the measurement of prices in France as an "explosive subject" (p. 6), as being "often a topical issue" (p. 3) and as a frequent object of "headlines" (ibid.) in the mass media.

In 2020, the same paradox persists, with flatlining inflation accompanied by fevered discussion of how it should be measured statistically. The evolution of the French consumer price index (CPI), which is the measure of inflation, is still closely scrutinised by households; it is the most frequently consulted indicator on the website of the French national statistics bureau 'INSEE' (Institut national de la statistique et des études économiques/Office of national statistics and economic studies) and at the same time has been monitored particularly closely by central banks ever since they adopted monetarist policies aimed at maintaining inflation at very low levels.

So why does the CPI attract so much attention? Because, for economic actors, the price index constitutes an 'expression of value'. Is the purchasing power of an individual wage or of that of a particular category of worker increasing or not? Is the currency appreciating or declining in value? Are transfer incomes going to rise or fall? Is the economy (as

[1] This book has been translated by Andrew Wilson.

measured by the rise in normal GDP deflated by the price index) growing? The disputes around the measurement of macroeconomic data are closely intertwined with theoretical disputes, including those around value theory. Throughout history, they have given rise to debates within the restrained world of statisticians. From time to time, simmering controversies erupt, underlining the sensitive nature of the topic.

A Constructed Datum

Like all macroeconomic indicators, the price index can elicit various responses. It might, for example, be regarded as a given, one bearing the seal of universality. A facile response of this kind confines the often 'daunting' questions that arise with regard to measurement of the price index to the strictly technical category (Vanoli 2002; Toutain 1996; Coyle 2014). Such a response also fosters a clear-cut division of labour conducive to a certain degree of efficiency in both academic research and the implementation of economic policies, with statisticians busying themselves with making technical improvements to the index while economists interpret and bring them into use and policymakers are tasked with reducing inflation.

However, such a response brings with it the risk of underestimating the controversies and conflicts around the definition and measurement of the cost of living and inflation, conflicts that are all the more likely to arise since the price index, like the cost of living indices, is an index that aggregates the general evolution of consumer prices and is consequently far from straightforward.

Another possible response is to objectify the confrontations and controversies, and more generally all the conventions on which measurement of the price index is based. This is the stance adopted in the present volume. It requires us to take seriously questions concerning the scope of the index and its weightings as well as how to deal with changes in the basket of products, including the introduction of new products, the substitution of products and the estimation of quality effects, all topics dealt with and discussed by many economists. In restoring to readers some of the keys to understanding what measurement of the evolution of prices encompasses, we are not seeking gratuitously to open the black box of measurement. Rather we are encouraging an interpretation in which it is shown that macroeconomic statistics—contrary to the process of naturalisation to which they are subjected—are the result of an "intense process of social construction" (Orléan 2004, p. 31; Porter 1995). In so doing, we are highlighting the risks that arise when the question that we have felt stirring in recent years is completely naturalised and depoliticised: after all, when we seek to determine whether the productive system serves the interests of the men and women who have contributed to it by improving quality of their lives, it is a societal question that is being addressed. The consumer price index is one of the key measures, but obviously not the only one, that is used to answer this question.

Thus the many controversies that have punctuated the French evolution of this compound measure are questions of political economy. They reflect changes on a number of different levels: changes in contemporary economic history resulting from the Europeanisation of economic affairs; changes in the particular socio-political relationship that governments maintain with macroeconomic indicators such as growth, productivity and inflation; and changes in the system of ideas that has seen advances in microeconomic theories of consumer behaviour and their utilitarian frameworks. These consumer behaviour theories have been a source of inspiration for successive reforms of the method of measuring the consumer price index. In these theories, the market becomes the legitimate space for the production of 'true' value. They are further strengthened by the generous support for this change provided by politicians and the media. And the final driver of change is INSEE's perpetual—and estimable—search for credibility.

Outline of the Book

The book analyses the internal conventions and the disputes—some of them tempestuous, others more muted—that have surrounded the measurement and use of the French consumer price index in official statistics. It shows how, as the controversies succeed one another, the CPI reflects like a mirror the ways in which the influence brought to bear by the various schools of thought and categories of actors has played out.

We begin in Chap. 1 with a presentation in statistical terms of the debates that continually re-erupt whenever the CPI comes under strong political pressure. Readers unfamiliar with writing on statistics will be able to skip this chapter. In Chap. 2 we review the CPI's Fordist period (1945–1970), which was characterised by a multiplicity of political pressures and ended in a sort of paroxysm with the publication by the major Trade Union affiliated to the communist party, the 'CGT', of an alternative indicator (1972–1998). These early historical phases ended with a major European turning point (Chap. 3) which, following the introduction of the Maastricht criteria and then the transition to the euro, transformed not only the political and economic context but also, with the introduction of the harmonised index of consumer prices (HICP) and the increased role played by Eurostat, the measure itself. The new focus on European integration and the increased circulation of mainstream ideas, revitalised by the emergence of neoliberal ideas in the USA, led eventually to a questioning of the very principle of a measure computed close to the market that was incapable of capturing the qualitative aspects of the evolution of consumption and production. Taking account of the question of product quality (Chap. 4), which focuses renewed attention on the incommensurability of individual preferences and utilities that Vilfredo Pareto had already highlighted, drove a wedge into the ideal of a public authority operating completely independently in order to produce objective measures. Chapter 5 examines the conflicts around definition, in particular that between a price index based on a constant basket of goods and services and a cost of living index, which is consubstantial with the long history of the price index; American statistics, which for a long time set the 'COGI' (cost of goods index) against the COLI (cost of living index), has now gone beyond this debate as far as official statistics are concerned (Stapleford 2009). For historical reasons specific to the France of the 1970s, INSEE maintains, at least in its communications, a strict division between a consumer price index and a cost of living index, as is the case in the European Union. In fact, however, the format of the data, the techniques employed and the dominance of utilitarian ideas are all factors that prefigure the possible advent of a constant utility index, the orthodox term for the cost of living index.

The purpose of Chap. 6 is to trace the reform of checkout data, with an emphasis on the shift it has produced in the boundaries between the public and private spheres in the process of constructing the CPI. The argument here is that the recent changes towards the use of checkout data constitute a modern expression of the reuse of private data by a public actor. Chapter 7 begs the question that runs through the whole book: is the CPI 'under-' or 'over'-estimated?

I am deeply grateful to the administrators and statisticians at INSEE as well as to the trade unionists, some of whom—often very generously—agreed to be interviewed in the course of this research, which is based in part on this field survey. It is thanks to these people that this book is able—at least I sincerely hope it is—to give an account of the debates, experiments and hesitations that have punctuated the life of the price index. They reflect not only the socio-political nature of the index but also, ultimately, the life of ideas just as much as the country's socio-economic and political life.

References

Coyle, D. 2014. *GDP: A Brief but Affectionate History*. Princeton: Princeton University Press.

Orléan, A. 2004. Analyse économique des conventions. Paris: PUF, coll. « Quadrige ».

Piriou, J.-P. 1992. *L'indice des prix*. 2e rééd. Paris: La Découverte, coll. « Repères ».

Porter, T. 1995. *Trust in Numbers: The Pursuit of Objectivity in Science and Public Life*. Princeton: Princeton University Press.

Stapleford Th., A. 2009. *The Cost of Living in America. A Political History of Economic Statistics 1880–2000*. Cambridge: Cambridge University Press.

Toutain, J.-C. 1996. Comparaisons entre les différentes évaluations du produit intérieur brut de la France de 1815 à 1938. Ou l'histoire économique quantitative a-t-elle un sens? *Revue économique* 47 (3): 893–919.

Vanoli, A. 2002. *Une histoire de la comptabilité nationale*. Paris: La Découverte, coll. « Repères », 655p.

CHAPTER 1

'What is a Price Index': Statistical Approach

1 Introduction

Every month, the French National Institute of Statistics and Economic Studies (INSEE) collects, thanks to a team of 200 price collectors, around 390,000 prices ('series') in two main ways. Some 200,000 of them are collected directly by investigators from a stratified sample of 30,000 points of sale that takes account of consumer behaviour. A further 190,000 prices (which INSEE calls 'tariffs' or 'rates') are collected directly by INSEE using a number of very different methodologies, to which we will return later. These prices are then gradually aggregated into a consumer price index.

Production of the CPI is a task that, together with the population census, is a major preoccupation for INSEE. The history of the price index is also very closely intertwined with that of INSEE. Given that the whole operation is conducted on a very large scale and that it is based on a long tradition of statistical rigour of which INSEE can be proud, it is hardly surprising that it uses up significant resources month after month (INSEE employs some 200 investigators distributed over the whole of France and around 100 so-called *gestionnaires-prix* or price technicians). The demands on INSEE are all the greater since the CPI is published each month and is never revised, unlike the EU's HICP or GDP.

Since the end of the 1970s, when Raymond Barre was prime minister of France, monetarist economic policies have gradually led inflation to be

F. Jany-Catrice, *A Political Economy of the Measurement of Inflation*,
https://doi.org/10.1007/978-3-030-59940-9_1

maintained at low levels. Nevertheless, inflation is still one of the most frequently consulted indices on INSEE's website, which is used in a general way by a wide range of people: the households of divorcees, whose maintenance is indexed to the CPI, the 10.6% of employees paid the national minimum wage in 2017 and whose pay increases in line with the evolution of the CPI calculated for the lowest quartile, national accountants and economists, who use it to deflate GDP and thus obtain a growth rate (GDP in volume terms) and the governor of the Banque de France, who has monitored inflation in minute detail since the 1970s.

Like the other macroeconomic aggregates, it was above all with the Keynesian policies introduced from the 1930s onwards that the notion of aggregate effective demand and those of households' standard of living and purchasing power came to the fore. Thus these Keynesian policies necessarily brought the general evolution of prices into the spotlight. This period also coincided with the advent of macroeconomics, which championed the notion that economies could be managed directly by manipulating these aggregates (Stapleford 2009, p. 383; Armatte 2010). But how is this inflation, assessed by the CPI, itself measured?

How does the language of statistics, which can be used to report on the general evolution of prices, bring price indices into the spotlight?

2 The Statistical Principle of a Price Index: Elementary Indices and Aggregation

The idea of using a composite index to measure the general evolution of prices established itself very early on. It is based on the realisation that an index that summarises in a single figure the totality of price changes must have a use, not solely to track the evolution of the macroeconomic dynamic that it is designed to reflect but also for other related purposes, in particular the indexation of expenditure or income to the evolution of prices.

2.1 *The Elementary Indices*

If consumption were reduced to a single good i, it would not be difficult to estimate the evolution of its price between times 0 and t. If, for example, the price of a loaf of bread increased from 90 pence in January 2002 to £1.20 in January 2016, we would say that the price of this particular good had increased by 33.3% [(1.20-0.9)/0.90], or by about 1.02% per year.

Statistically, this calculation can be written thus:

$$\Delta pi = \left(\frac{pi_t - pi_0}{pi_0} \right) \tag{1.1}$$

But how do we go about accounting statistically for the evolution of the price of a 'basket' of goods that is made up not solely of bread but also of clothes, consumer durables and services?

In this case, it is not so much the level of the basket's price that is important but rather its evolution. This is why an elementary price index is used in statistics. In the previous example, we would say that the price index of the loaf of bread in January 2016 was 133.3 ($1.2/0.9 = 1.333 \times 100$), base 100 in January 2002.

Generally, and in accordance with the notation (1.1) above, the elementary price index for good i between 0 and t (notated $I(p)_{t/0}$) or, more precisely, the price of good I at time t, base 100 in 0, is (Δp_i - 1) × 100, or:

$$I(pi)_{t/0} = \frac{pi_t}{pi_0} \times 100 \tag{1.2}$$

the value of the elementary indices is that they serve as normalisers (the average of variations in heterogeneous goods with different prices can, after all, be worked out) and thus facilitate aggregation by making it possible to use an average (for the moment we will be using the arithmetic mean) and a weighting coefficient.

If the basket is made up of k goods i, varying from 1 to k, one possibility, although not the only one, is to construct a price index as the arithmetic mean of the elementary indices.

$$I(p)_{t/0} = \sum_{i=1}^{k} xi\, I(pi)_{t/0} \tag{1.3}$$

where xi = the weighting allocated to the variation in the price of each good.

Conventionally, a base or reference year is adopted (in our case, it would be 0, the initial year, adopted as a simplified convention). In order to estimate the evolution of goods over a period, the calculations do, after all, have to be carried out without modifying the structure of the goods making up the basket, otherwise the variations will reflect something quite different from the variations in price, namely the variations in the quality of the good or even changes in the structure of consumption. Thus the idea is to keep the basket of goods constant. Statisticians say they work with a fixed basket of goods from a specific base or reference year.

2.2 *Aggregating the Elementary Indices*

The difficulty in aggregating the elementary indices is to find the best weighting coefficient in order to produce a differentiated account of a strong (or weak) variation of a little (or widely) consumed good. The share of the goods consumed expressed in volume terms cannot be used, since goods sold in diverse units would have to be summed (units of loaves of bread and units of rent or cinema tickets). Since 1946, when INSEE first had at its disposal robust family budget surveys (Desrosières 2003), the contemporary version of which dates from 1979, it has been the budget coefficient that has been adopted as the weighting coefficient. Each good is allocated a weighting that represents the share of total household expenditure given over to its consumption as revealed by this quinquennial survey. This intuitive choice, made possible by the unifying role of money, also enables the price index to be consistent with national accounts data. In absolute terms, however, the choice of this budget coefficient is not the only possible one. In some studies, for example, frequency of purchase is preferred, particularly as a means of interpreting perceptions of inflation (we will return to this point in Chap. 3).

The budget coefficient ωi of a good i is the share (proportion) of expenditure on this good (di) in total expenditure. It is expressed thus:

$$\omega i = \frac{di}{\sum di} \tag{1.4}$$

with Σdi = D, total expenditure, and d_i = expenditure on good i.

By bringing together (1.3) and (1.4), the price index of a basket of goods i of price pi can be expressed thus:

$$I(p)_{t/0} = \sum_{i=1}^{k} \omega_i I(pi)_{t/0} \tag{1.5}$$

The base or reference year to be used in calculating the price index has still to be chosen. On the face of it, statisticians have two options: they can adopt either the base year (0) or the current year (t). The reference is extremely important and, as we shall see in Chap. 2, each major generation of INSEE indices brings with it a change of reference year as well as reforms of the index. INSEE takes advantage of the establishment of these new generations in order to tidy up its index or even to introduce methodological changes, some of which have been significant. Historically, certain changes of base year have been very controversial (as in 1957, see Sect. 3.1). Others, which nevertheless constituted major reforms, were less contentious (this was the case with the 2015 change of base year). Since the end of the 1970s, the European Union has required the base year to be updated every five years, in order to prevent the index's consumption structure from becoming too out of date and to ensure that changes of base year take place in all member states at the same time.

Furthermore, while the arithmetic mean has some fine mathematical properties, it is not the only possible choice. A wide range of averages are used in statistics, including the geometric mean (very useful, particularly for calculating average annual growth rates) and the harmonic mean (used to find the average of certain rates). The diversity of possible choices is evident from the diversity of price and quantity indices that are available. And it is to these that we now turn.

3 The Various Possible Measures: Laspeyres, Paasche, Fisher

3.1 The Laspeyres Price Index

Although the origins of statistical indices are sometimes said in the literature to lie in a book on 'the troubles brought about by the Napoleonic Wars' published by the Englishman Joseph Lowe in 1822, it was at the end of the nineteenth century with the so-called marginal revolution in economic thought that the concept of index numbers was developed, notably by authors such as Etienne Laspeyres and Williams Jevons (Neiburg 2011).

The Laspeyres price index is a composite index that is an arithmetic mean of the elementary indices of the variation in the prices of the goods *i*, weighted by the budget coefficients for the base year of each good considered (see Box 1.1).

Box 1.1 The Various Formulations of the Laspeyres Price Index

The Laspeyres price index is a composite index that is an arithmetic mean of the elementary indices of the variation in the prices of the goods *i*, weighted by the budget coefficients for the base year of each good considered. It is written thus:

$$L(p)_{t/0} = \sum_{i=1}^{k} \omega_{i0} I(pi)_{t/0}$$

This average can be written in two other ways. The first of these is mathematical: by replacing ω_0 and $I(p)_{t/0}$ by their respective values, that is $\omega_{i0} = \frac{p_{i0}q_{i0}}{\sum_{i=1}^{k} p_{i0}q_{i0}}$ and $I(p_i)_{t/0} = \frac{p_{it}}{p_{i0}} \times 100$, a different formulation of the Laspeyres index is obtained:

$$L(p)_{t/0} = \frac{\sum_{i=1}^{k} pi_t qi_0}{\sum_{i=1}^{k} pi_0 qi_0} \times 100$$

In order to explain this ratio in economic terms, a line of reasoning based on total expenditure can be developed. Put simply, total expenditure in the base year is the sum of the quantities of goods *i* purchased in that base year to which is allocated the price *i* of that same year.

$$D_0 = \sum_{i=1}^{k} pi_0 qi_0$$

The computation of a Laspeyres price index can be regarded as a measure of the structural evolution of total expenditure; a Laspeyres price index gives a picture of what would have happened if, in the evolution of total expenditure (D_0), only the prices had varied, leaving the quantities unchanged. The fictitious total expenditure can be written thus:

$D_t = \sum_{i=1}^{k} pi_t qi_0$. This is the expense that consumers would have had to bear if prices *alone* had varied.

Thus a Laspeyres price index can be written as the ratio of total expenditure at the base period to this fictitious expenditure:

$$L(p)_{t/0} = \frac{D_t}{D_0} = \frac{\sum_{i=1}^{k} pi_t qi_0}{\sum_{i=1}^{k} pi_0 qi_0} \times 100$$

The value of a statistical presentation of this kind is that it highlights the important idea that, in order to compute a Laspeyres price index, statistical data are required on (i) the quantities at the base period and (ii) the prices at the base period and at the current period. In other words, all that is necessary to compute a synthetic index of this kind is the annual collection of prices. Furthermore, by comparing the numerator and the denominator, it can be seen that this is indeed a measure of the variation in prices between 0 and *t*, since in this formulation only *p* varies.

Let us take a quantified example of a basket made up of three elementary products: besides the ten loaves of bread consumed every month, it contains four cinema tickets (elementary price £6.7 in 2002 and £9.0 in 2016) and a monthly bus ticket (elementary price £55.0 in 2002, £70 in 2016). In this example, total monthly expenditure in 2002 was £90.8, made up of £9 (a budget coefficient of 10%) spent on bread, £26.8 (a budget coefficient of 30%) on cinema tickets and £55 (a budget coefficient of 61%) on the monthly bus ticket. By allocating these budget coefficients to the goods' elementary price indices, a price index of £128.9 is obtained for the basket in accordance with the Laspeyres formula. In other words, the price of the basket rose by 28.9% over the period as a whole, or by 1.8% per year on average (Table 1.1).

This extremely conventional but also very practical way of computing the index is relatively less expensive than other conventions because it requires only collection of the elementary prices, provided it is assumed that the method can take a base year as its starting point. However, it is not the only possible convention.

3.2 *The Paasche Price Index*

The fictitious expenditure can also be calculated by varying the quantities rather than the prices, the aim now being to estimate the total expense consumers would have to bear if only the quantities varied and not the prices.

$$\check{D}t = \sum_{i=1}^{k} pi_0 qi_t$$

The Paasche index (named after its originator, Hermann Paasche) was developed both as a harmonic mean of the elementary price indices (i), weighted by the budget coefficient for the current year (rather than the base year), and as a ratio of the total expenditure at the current time to the fictitious expenditure if only the quantities varied (ii).

Thus the Paasche price index can be expressed as a harmonic mean of the elementary price indices weighted by the budget coefficients for the current year (see Box 1.2). In our previous quantified example, the Paasche price index for the basket of goods turns out to be 124.8, a price increase of 24.8% or an average annual increase of 1.6%. Thus depending on the conventions used to compute it, the price index in our example increases by 24.8% (Paasche) or by 29.9% (Laspeyres).

This representation, which is equally conventional, is in fact less practical, since it requires the current year's prices (known as 'current prices') to be collected, as well as the quantities for the current year. It is costly to gather data on the quantities consumed since they are derived from household budgets. Thus it is more constraining and for that reason has often been put aside.

Table 1.1 Computing a Laspeyres price index

Goods in the basket	*Price of the good (£)*		*Quantities of the good*	*Expenditure on the good (£)*	*Good's budget coefficient (in %)*	*Good's elementary price index*	*Laspeyres price index*
	2002	*2016*	*2002*	*2002*		*I(p)t/0 × 100*	$L(p)_{t/0} = \sum_{i=1}^{k} \omega_{i0} I(pi)_{t/0}$
Loaf of bread	0.9	1.2	10	9	9.9	122.2	12.1
Cinema	6.7	9.1	4	26.8	29.5	134.3	39.6
Monthly bus ticket	55	70	1	55	60.6	127.3	77.1
Total				90.8	100		128.9

Box 1.2 The Various Formulations of the Paasche Price Index

The Paasche price index is expressed as an average of the elementary price indices weighted by the budget coefficients for the current year, which is summarised in the following formula:

$$P(p)_{t/0} = \frac{1}{\sum_{i=1}^{k} \frac{\omega_{it}}{I(p)_{t/0}}} \times 100$$

The version of the Paasche index presented below, in which the numerator shows that the budget reference year is the current year (t), is fairly easily obtained by replacing ω_1 and $I(p)_{t/0}$ by their respective values, that is $\omega_{it} = \frac{p_{it}q_{it}}{\sum_{i=1}^{k} p_{it}q_{it}}$ and $I(p_i)_{t/0} = \frac{p_{it}}{p_{i0}} \times 100$. In this formulation, similarly, only the prices vary (p_t in the numerator and p_0 in the denominator), which once again shows that what this formulation is attempting to estimate is the 'pure' price effect:

$$P(p)_{t/0} = \frac{\sum_{i=1}^{k} pi_t qi_t}{\sum_{i=1}^{k} pi_0 qi_t} \times 100$$

In fact, the pure evolution of the prices is never obtained, since other variations appear as the values vary, but we will return to this in later chapters.

This time $P(p)_{t/0}$ can also be written as an expenditure report.

$$P(p)_{t/0} = \frac{D_t}{\overset{ç}{D}_t}$$

in which $D_t = \sum_{i=1}^{k} pi_t qi_t$ and $\overset{ç}{D}_t = \sum_{i=1}^{k} pi_0 qi_t$

The statistics literature also suggests that a Laspeyres price index tends to overestimate the general evolution of prices. And indeed, if the consumption structure is maintained unchanged for several years, then substitution effects linked to the variation in prices between goods over the period may be underestimated (if consumption switches towards the goods whose prices rise the least). The Paasche price index, conversely, is said to underestimate the general evolution of prices because it underweights goods subject to high price inflation. These remarks are valid only if the fixed basket of goods is not regarded as the optimal index for measuring the 'cost of living' (see Chap. 5).

3.3 The Fisher Price Index

The early twentieth-century economist and mathematician, Irving Fisher, is known "not only for theoretical and technical developments relating to the measurement of prices but also for the invention of index numbers and their transformation into public data by producing, selling and converting them into commodities" (Neiburg 2011). Neiburg explains how Fisher set up a "consultancy bureau" that "circulated among its clients printed sheets with tables and indices showing the variations in some of the principal prices in the economy, thereby introducing into the economic public space in North America a new type of information that rapidly changed the agenda of the business papers" (op. cit. p. 38).

In the course of his work as an academic, Fisher developed an index that is sometimes regarded as the best (or superlative) index and which takes the unweighted average of the Laspeyres and Paasche indices. It is written as follows:

$$F(p)_{1/0} = \sqrt[2]{L(p)_{1/0} P(p)_{1/0}}$$

This formula has the advantage of being the geometric mean of the two indices, which limits the effects of statistical over and underestimation; at the same time, it has the major disadvantage of the Paasche indices, namely that it requires the collection of data on quantities for the current period.

3.4 *The Missing Properties of the Synthetic Indices*

The elementary price indices have numerous properties, including the fact of being chainable, reversible and transitive. However, this is not the case for most of the synthetic indices and is particularly not the case for the Laspeyres or Paasche indices. In economic terms, this means that a comparison of two dates depends a great deal on the base adopted. It also means that an index can be used only to compare the two periods to which it refers. In theory, if a price index base 100 in 1998 rose by 25.8%, for example, between 1998 and 2015 and by 26.0% between 1998 and 2015, we cannot strictly speaking draw any conclusions from the index about the evolution of prices between 2015 and 2016. It would, after all, be easy to demonstrate that for any $0 < t' < t$, generally, $L(p)_{t/0} \neq L(p)_{t/t'} . L(p)_{t'/0}$.

The same applies to the Paasche index, unlike the Fisher index, which has this property of circularity but which requires, as we have seen, significantly more data than a Laspeyres index. It is also less easy to interpret than a Laspeyres index. This is particularly problematic for the economic analysis of inflation.

This arithmetic of the consumer price indices has obvious pedagogical virtues. However, it tells us little about the conventions and disputes—some of them muted—surrounding the measurement and uses of the price index in official statistics that reveal the extent to which the CPI has always been aimed at those in power, with a specific objective in mind, and not just at observers wishing to equip themselves with a disembodied tool in order to aid their observation. This indicator has some similarities with what the historian Michel Armatte says of mathematical objects: "Far from being a stable nomadic object, journeying alone through the world, it is permanently subject to changes, reinterpretations and a variety of different, frequently competing social uses" (Armatte 2010, p. 9). In the final analysis, the multiple exercises in interpretation that are an inherent part of constructing a price index, the experimentation, the conventions and controversies as well as the reforms of the methods of computation remain relatively unknown. It is partly its tumultuous history, to which we are going to return throughout the book, that has made the CPI an "opaque object" (Lemoine 2016, p. 296). Knowledge of its origins, its morphology and the changes it has undergone is all the more necessary since the CPI, besides being a product of the theoretical, socio-political and symbolic principles underlying it, also produces effects.

4 Implementing Price Indices Both Statistically and Practically

We will confine ourselves here to some of the statistical changes the CPI has undergone that have taken it away to some extent from its original purpose, that is measurement of the evolution of the price of a basket of goods and services whose composition remains constant and standard over time. These reforms (the use of a chain index and of geometric means and the various measures of quality), to which we will return throughout the book, were driven by a range of different factors. Firstly, they arose out of the practical impossibility of maintaining a fixed basket of goods over a long period, which was Laspeyres' theoretical plan, because of the variability of economic practices in markets. Some goods disappear while others emerge and prices fluctuate significantly during the observation period for various reasons linked to seasonality, fashion trends, speculation or even strategic pricing policies (such as yield pricing, which is the practice of charging different prices to different customers in order to manage capacity while maximising revenues). Secondly, these reforms can be interpreted as a gradual shift away from the CPI towards a cost of living index, that is to say (if we provisionally adopt the standard economic definition of the cost of living) an index that can measure the evolution of the minimum expenditure required to maintain a certain standard living or a standard level of well-being. This will be examined in greater detail in Chaps. 5 and 7.

4.1 Chain Indices

Price indices, whether they be of the Laspeyres, Paasche or Fisher variant, are very sensitive to the base period adopted, as already noted above. The choice of base period is crucial and may permanently alter the results if a major event took place around the base year. For example, at the time of the change of base in 1957, the then French president of the council, Paul Ramadier, observed that the new index was 104.5, while the previous one had been only 102.3. "Francis-Louis Closon explained that many items that did not feature in the 213-item index were included in the new index and that they were individually of a higher than average value" (Touchelay 1993).

Above all, while it is convenient to work with a base year, the very real contingencies (changes in individuals' lifestyles and hence in the structure of consumption) mean that the base year has to be updated regularly in order to prevent the index from becoming out of date.

Since 1971 and the switch to the 295-item basket, INSEE has computed and edited a chain-linked Laspeyres index in order to construct a price index that reflects household consumption as closely as possible but which is consequently at some distance from a fixed-basket price index. This pragmatic innovation was introduced in order to update the structure of consumption annually and to ensure that the inter-period comparisons were constructed and hence that the index retained its transitivity. Thus the budget coefficients are revised every year using national accounting data which, in the case of Laspeyres index, removes the advantage of the index's fixed weightings. Roughly speaking, the chain-linked index (CI) is computed as follows (for any $0 < t' < t$): $IC(p)_{t/0} = L(p)_{t/t'} L(p)_{t'/0}$.

The index's transitivity is maintained by these annually revised weightings (for the record: $L(p)_{t/t'}$ has the budget coefficient $\omega_{t'}$ while $L(p)_{t'/0}$ has the budget coefficient ω_0).

4.2 *The Geometric Means of the Micro Price Indices*

Aggregation by the Laspeyres index involves consumption items that are already largely aggregated (e.g. food). This aggregation has also to be conducted at the level of the 'varieties', the most detailed goods. The Laspeyres format cannot be used at these levels of detail because the budget coefficients are not available at this level. Aggregation at the detailed level of the goods has from the outset been carried out on the basis of a simple, unweighted arithmetic mean of the micro-indices that are used to compute the price index. This aggregative format, which is used for homogeneous items, is sometimes called the Dutot index. These indices can also be computed using geometric means. Long eschewed by statisticians, the use of geometric means is now advised in the international manuals, notably that produced by the ILO et al. (2004); this can be attributed to the concerted efforts of the experts fighting to have the method adopted (see following chapters). It has even been in use in the production of the French CPI since the beginning of the 1990s for the computation of certain micro price indices for heterogeneous varieties. These unweighted geometric means of micro-indices are also called Jevons index.

They have the following arithmetic structure: $J(a)_{t/0} = \prod_{i=1}^{k} \left(\frac{p_i^t}{p_i^0} \right)^{\frac{1}{k}}$, where *J*(*a*) is the Jevons price index weighted for the elementary aggregate *a* and *k* the number of products *i* in the elementary aggregate *a*. The purpose of using Jevons index is to take account of substitution effects in household consumption strategies. After all, if they are free and rational, consumers will, according to the theory, purchase the goods that have become relatively less expensive but provide the same utility, to the detriment of others that have become more expensive. Fixed-basket indices (Laspeyres, Paasche) cannot take account of this substitution effect; the use of geometric means seeks partly to attenuate this effect and generally leads to the price increase as calculated with the arithmetic being reduced *mechanically*. However, this marks a shift away from a price index as an indicator of the general evolution of the prices of a fixed basket of goods towards an index that is closer to households' purchasing practices and cost of living as represented in microeconomic theory (see Chaps. 5 and 7).

4.3 *Quantities, Volumes and Pure Prices*

It is convenient, both statistically and pedagogically, to set out the indices on the basis of these formulas. They are rigorous and make it possible to expound more or less complex mathematical arguments. Nevertheless, they take no account whatsoever of one of the most thorny problems in price statistics, namely that of quality. Until now, it has been assumed that expenditure combines a price effect and a quantity effect: $D_t = \sum_{i=1}^{k} pi_t qi_t$. From a dynamic perspective, this means that the variation in values (here expenditure) combines a price variation and quantity variation.

However, since the 1960s, economic arguments have stated more precisely that the variation in value (va) combines a variation in price (*p*), a variation in quantity (*q*) and a variation in quality (ql) (Box 1.3).

This could be written in this form: $\delta va = \delta p \times \delta q \times \delta ql$.

In the example of the price of the loaf of bread already set out above, it was stated that the price of the loaf had increased from 90 pence to £1.20 between 2002 and 2016. Before thinking of a pure price rise, this may be linked to the fact that its weight had risen from 250 g to 280 g (or had

Box 1.3 From Value to Volumes in the History of National Accounting
Until the 1950s, according to André Vanoli, national accountant and author of a comprehensive survey of the history of national accounting (*L'Histoire de la Comptabilité nationale*), statisticians had little interest in variations in volume (Vanoli 2002, pp. 466–467) but were more interested in variations in the value of macroeconomic variables. It was not until the first bouts of high inflation in the post-war period that economists began to turn their attention to variations in volume (GDP) or in real terms (income). From the early 1960s onwards, the decomposition of a variation in value of an aggregate into a price variation and a volume variation gained in legitimacy. This approach, explains Vanoli, "is based on the idea that, in all flows, there is an explicit or implicit 'contract' between economic agents. In all cases, volume then becomes the counterpart in money within the price system of the base year in which the contract is 'physically' executed with the aim of providing a certain degree of satisfaction" (Vanoli op. cit., p. 479). An initial attempt to generalise the price-volume breakdowns was made in the French national accounts in 1957, but "the experiment was not followed up. Too many flows are impervious to the volume-price breakdown" (Vanoli, op. cit., p. 480).

decreased to 200 g), which would mean that we were dealing with a quantity effect. If the loaf now weighs only 200 g—as we can experience from time to time as consumers—then the price of the loaf will not be said to have risen by 33.3% between 2002 and 2016 but by 33.3% + the loss of quantity. The price of a 250 g loaf will have risen from 90 p to £1.50, a rise of 66.7%.

It may also be that the price of the loaf has risen because the dough is now organic or has had sesame seeds added or is now leavened (or conversely more industrial, tray baked, etc.). Now we are dealing with a quality effect (positive or negative). Once these two effects have been captured and neutralised, which in the case of quality poses a whole heap of problems that are examined in Chap. 4, it is the residual that is regarded as a 'pure price' and which is recorded as a price variation in the CPI (see Box 1.4).

Box 1.4 'Pure Prices'

The notion of a 'pure price' suggests that all that remains in the goods traded is a quantitative relationship, a sort of "hidden magnitude" (Orléan 2004) that has only to be rid of various noises or random fluctuations (it is in this sense that differences of a qualitative nature have been neutralised in a pure price). The pure price's theoretical environment is that of a competitive price regime that disregards monopolistic forms of competition and the existence of regulated prices (tariffs), administered prices (agreements or understandings, cartels) and prices subject to high levels of speculation (whose share is increasing). It also takes little account of the differentiated pricing practices embodied in the notion of *yield management*, that ultra-flexible pricing strategy that aims to maximise operators' margins by personalising (or individualising) prices and which has become established through close surveillance of consumers' willingness of pay. *Yield management* has led to fluctuating prices on the railways, in air travel, in the hotel industry and in on-demand platforms such as Uber. It is rather comical to note that the closer pricing practices are to theory (yield management is based directly on consumer theory), the more difficult it is for official statistics to track them in a statistically coherent manner.

The notion of the pure price is also found in the concept of core inflation, and indicator which, according to INSEE, seeks to reflect the underlying trends in the evolution of prices. It is said to be free of the "noises" (Silver 2006) generated by administered prices 'subject to state intervention (electricity, gas, tobacco etc.)' and 'products with volatile prices (petroleum products, fresh produce, dairy products, meat, flowers and plants etc.)'. According to advocates of the notion of core inflation, it contains only real variations in price that result from the evolution of real magnitudes. As far as these measurements are concerned, the state is regarded as a disruptive element compared with the purity of the market prices that are to be retranscribed.

Why is this variation in quality not taken into account in the Laspeyres and Paasche indices? The first reason is that price theory is based on the assumption that the set of goods whose price is being investigated is of constant quality. In other words, the Laspeyres and Paasche indices are valid provided that the quality of the goods that make up the basket remains constant over time. The second reason is that statisticians use a concept that combines the notion of quantity and that of quality, which they call 'volume' (*vo*).

Thus what we are proposing to write thus: $\delta va = \delta p \times \delta q \times \delta ql$ is set out in the handbooks as follows: $\delta va = \delta p \times \delta vo$.

This transformation has the advantage of making it possible to rediscover the indices' initial format. Strictly speaking, a Laspeyres index should be interpreted as follows:

$$L(p)_{t/0} = \frac{\sum_{i=1}^{k} pi_t voi_0}{\sum_{i=1}^{k} pi_0 voi_0}$$

where *voi* (the volume of the good) has replaced *qi* (the quantity of good *i*).

The equation seeks to keep at arm's length the notion of quality, whose normative character and the value judgements that accompany it are always particularly awkward to put into practice statistically, particularly when dealing with fields linked to macroeconomics.

While it maintains the idea of a possible calculability space that could also take account of quality, this decomposition delegates to other bodies the task of dealing with the singular nature of production and trade and the incommensurable nature of quality, which here is completely absorbed into a hybrid entity called volume. Moreover, the choice of the term 'volume' is in keeping with the idea of the expansion of statistical "robustness" (Gayon and Lemoine 2014). To the uninitiated, however, it might appear deceptive, since it tilts more towards quantity than towards quality. Who among the users of statistics knows that changes in volume encompass variations in quality? Ultimately, this is linked to the difficulty of answering the question: quality for whom? According to what points of reference? A whole chapter (Chap. 4) is given over to this thorny but fundamental question.

5 The Composition of the Price Index and the Evolution of the CPI over Time

Thus the official general consumer price index is an index that inclines towards the Laspeyres type, weighted as it is by the budget coefficients for the base year. In 2016, the relative shares of the budget coefficients were determined on the new 2015 base, the eighth generation of the price index. It can be seen that food accounts for 16% of household consumption in the index, manufactures for 27% and services for almost half (48%) (Table 1.2).

The INSEE data also show the evolution of the average annual growth of the CPI over the long term. The elegant graph below highlights the very high (hyperinflationary even) rates of inflation that characterised the immediate post-war period (between 1945 and 1952), the following period of greater stability (except for 1968) that lasted until the beginning of the 1970s, the period in which the state apparatus began to be reformed: in the name of inflation, the state as banker began to be dismantled.

Table 1.2 The CPI budget coefficients in France, 2016

	Share in household consumption (%)
Food	16
Fresh products	2
Food excl. fresh products	14
Manufactured products	27
Clothing and footwear	4
Health products	5
Other manufactured products	18
Energy	8
Petroleum products	4
Services	48
Rent, water and household waste disposal	8
Health services	6
Transport	3
Communications	2
Other services	29
Tobacco	2

Scope: France as a whole, all households

Source: Insee, consumer price index base 2015

Fig. 1.1 Evolution of the CPI's average annual rate of increase between 1945 and 2017 (in %), France as a whole. (Scope: CPI Parisian series until 1962, urban households until 1992, metropolitan France from 1993 onwards, France as a whole since 1999). Source: Insee (2017)

The highly inflationary period between 1972 and 1984 gave way to a period in which inflation was brought under control and maintained at a very low level. These developments will be examined in detail in the following chapters (Fig. 1.1).

References

Armatte, M. 2010. *La science économique comme ingénierie. Quantification et modélisation*. Paris: Presses des Mines, Mines ParisTech, coll. « Sciences sociales ».

Desrosières, A. 2003. Du travail à la consommation: l'évolution des usages des enquêtes sur le budget des familles. *Journal de la société statistique de Paris*, tome 144, n° 1–2: 75–111.

Gayon, V., and B. Lemoine. 2014. Maintenir l'ordre économique. Politiques de désencastrement et de réencastrement de l'économie. *Politix*, 2014/1, n° 105: 7–35.

ILO/IMF/OECD/UNECE/Eurostat/The World Bank. 2004. *Consumer price index manual: Theory and practice*. Geneva: International Labour Office.

Lemoine, B. 2016. *L'ordre de la dette*. Paris: La Découverte.

Neiburg, F. 2011. La guerre des indices. L'inflation au Brésil 1964–1994. *Genèses*, 2011/3, n° 84: 25–46.

Orléan, A. 2004. Analyse économique des conventions. Paris: PUF, coll. « Quadrige ».

Silver, M. 2006. Core Inflation Measures and Statistical Issues in Choosing Among Them. *IMF Working Paper*, April.

Stapleford Th., A. 2009. *The Cost of Living in America. A Political History of Economic Statistics 1880–2000*. Cambridge: Cambridge University Press.

Touchelay, B. 1993. *L'Insee des origines à 1961: évolution et relation avec la réalité économique, politique et sociale*. thèse d'histoire, Paris 12.

Vanoli, A. 2002. *Une histoire de la comptabilité nationale*. Paris: La Découverte, coll. « Repères », 655p.

CHAPTER 2

A Political Economy of the Price Index 1913–1990

1 Introduction

The early versions of the CPI in France at the beginning of the twentieth century were based on measurement of a basket of 13 items widely consumed in Paris (calculated monthly, base 100 July 1914) and "in every provincial town or city with more 100 inhabitants and in six regions (calculated monthly, base 100 August 1914" (Touchelay 2003, p. 3)). The aim then was simply to have a point of reference for the cost of purchasing a basket of commonly consumed items, based on the consumption expenditure of families with modest incomes. "The individuals questioned were selected from among the investigators' acquaintances", writes Touchelay, and family expenditure was noted in an accounts book for a week (op. cit.) (Table 2.1).

Very soon, however, this price index was not only modelled and transformed but also put under pressure. The purpose of this chapter is to give an account of these changes on the basis of the following chronology. An initial period of experimentation, which ran until the inter-war period, laid the pragmatic foundations for a price index. The period of the Second World War was marked by the power of the welfare state and the power conferred on economic planning. The 1970s and, above all, the year 1980 marked a significant turning point in the index's history. On the one hand, technocratic expertise acquired greater legitimacy, thereby creating an intellectual climate conductive to the promotion, first in the USA and later

F. Jany-Catrice, *A Political Economy of the Measurement of Inflation*, https://doi.org/10.1007/978-3-030-59940-9_2

Table 2.1 Composition of the 13-item index

Items	*Items*
Bread	Potatoes
Fresh meat	Pulses
Pork	Sugar
Butter	Cooking oil
Eggs	Paraffin
Milk	Methylated spirits
Cheese	

Source: (Touchelay 2003), based on P. Delain, G. Laurent, B. Terrat, *Les statistiques de prix en France et en divers pays étrangers*. Insee, Imprimerie nationale, 1953

in France, of utilitarian frameworks. On the other hand, monetarist policies and, more generally, the financialisation of the economy impacted directly on efforts to rein in inflation. Besides the fact that, for historical reasons, inflation remained a sore point in Germany and that this anxiety was conveyed to decision-makers within the European Union, monetary stability was necessary in a system that sought to guarantee returns to savers who purchased debt (Lemoine 2016). These monetarist policies also impacted on the measurement of inflation.

Box 2.1 Prices and Economic Policy
Analysis of the measurement of prices and of the disputes that have surrounded it is revealing of the economic debates that have set two approaches against each other since the early days of political economy. This same tension is evident in the computation of the index, with advocates of a method of measurement and public intervention at some remove from the market based on the legitimacy of the state facing off against champions of the sovereignty of individual choices as expressed through the market with its capacity for self-regulation. The latter have become inextricably associated with the notion that there are two disconnected spheres, one monetary, the other real. In order for individual choices to be made in a state of perfect information, real value and monetary value have to evolve together. This position, which is the basis of the standard theory, postulates that the

(*continued*)

Box 2.1 (continued)

market automatically reveals agents' preferences, thereby ensuring optimal compatibility with their wishes. The crucial importance attached to low or zero inflation seeks to prevent market prices drifting away from the real value of the goods and services being exchanged. It is only on this condition that the price of the various goods perfectly measures the service rendered to users in terms of the quality and utility associated with consumption of these goods and services. Keynes, who initiated macroeconomic theories of aggregate demand, did not support the idea of market transparency and the market's self-balancing capacity. In his view, the economy was, on the contrary, primarily monetary and while markets were efficient in bringing agents together, they did not have the capacity to tell the truth. Historically, therefore, the macroeconomic approach has required an extensive statistical apparatus managed by the state that provides a clear picture of the major economic aggregates and enables the state to make the fine adjustments that the market is, from this point of view, incapable of making.

2 The Emergence of a Price Index: Between Proxy for Industrial Activity and Guarantee of Purchasing Power

The historical approach adopted here has heuristic value. It reveals the bases of the dynamics—some complementary, others contradictory—that are still at work today: one is the representation of wealth, the principle at work in particular when statistics focus on the quantification of qualities, another is redistribution, the principle at work when price indices are used as a direct or indirect benchmark for indexing wages, welfare benefits, etc. Can we speak of historical controversy? It has to be said that the few authors who have examined inflation from the point of view of the origins of its measurement do not seem to accord the same importance to these two principles.

The INSEE statistician Jean Rouchet (2016) considers the starting point for the construction and use of a retail price index in official statistics at the time of the American financial crisis of 1907. According to Rouchet, it was this crisis that gave rise to the construction of a proxy for economic activity: this proxy was the measurement of prices. In his view, the 1907 financial crisis in Wall Street led to a crisis in the real economy that brought about a sharp drop in output and imports. According to Alfred Sauvy, this initially American crisis "disturbed the public authorities" in France (Rouchet 2016, p. 5). The first price indices were conceived as indirect representations of economic activity, since it is easier to collect data on price changes than on volumes. Thus according to the historian, the first empirical estimates of prices carried out by official statisticians date from before the periods of inflation crises. This led to the first observatory of prices managed by Duge de Bernonville. Michel Huber—quoted by the authors—explained that the remit was to organise the collection of indices "that might serve as early warnings of general economic crises", further specifying that "the objective is certainly to measure economic activity [...] not inflation".

In his long-run statistical study, Rouchet provides a graph that suggests inflation was virtually zero before 1914. According to him, it was not until after the First World War, when prices had been increased fourfold, that serious consideration was given to putting a figure on inflation. At that point inflation became a public problem and the first indices in France were officially compiled: wholesale prices, then retail prices and finally industrial producer prices. It was the fixed-base Laspeyres index that was adopted in France, as it was in most other European countries and the USA. There were two reasons for this. One was practical: this was the least complicated—and least expensive—way of gathering data on the evolution of prices, as was noted in Chap. 1. The other was more conceptual. Lucien March was still director of the SGF (General Statistics Office) after the war, at the time when his prices department, "whose job it was to monitor the economic indices and to inform the government of what they were foretelling", was also playing a decisive role "in drawing up the economic recovery programme" (Armatte 2005, p. 3). For March: "A price index, that is to say the cost of a standard lifestyle" "is to be understood not in the popular sense but in the sense of being a tool for accurately measuring the effect of changes in the prices of things, independently of changes in habits or tastes or any increase in or differentiation of needs" (March 1911, p. 12, quoted by Rouchet op. cit.).

This historical perspective is not accepted unanimously. The historian Béatrice Touchelay, for her part, suggests that the price index actually appeared at the same time as "the first sudden upsurge in inflation" at the beginning of the twentieth century. According to Touchelay, it was intended "to appease the angry households that had risen up against the high cost of living three years earlier" (1993). The outlines of a 13-item retail price index can be found as early as 1913, with the first publication in 1916 (see Table 1.2).

Jean Moden tells a similar story in the case of Belgium. He shows that it was the Belgian Ministry of Labour that constructed the first price indices because "the labour organisations [...] were demanding in particular that they should be guaranteed a purchasing power equivalent to that workers enjoyed before hostilities broke out" (Moden 1982, p. 7). The first Belgian index was, furthermore, computed by 'a commission on the high cost of living'. Wage indexing was introduced in the Belgian mining industry from 1920 onwards, when the miners' joint national commission linked miners' wages to the evolution of the price index (Moden, op. cit., p. 8). The establishment in France, from 1919 onwards, of joint cost of living commissions in each of the *départements*, supervised by a 'Central Commission for Research on the Cost of Living' (CCERCV, decree of 1920)' (Chélini 1998, p. 24), reflected the increasing importance for governments and households of concerning themselves with the cost of living. These commissions were tasked with compiling a range of standard budgets with the aim of calculating the cost of living of typical working-class households. American historians also have shown that anger at the increase in the cost of living dates in North America from the beginning of the twentieth century. However, according to Thomas Stapleford (2009), author of a major book entitled *The Cost of Living in America*, this anger did not immediately arouse interest in retail price indicators. Attention was focused rather on trusts and monopolies, which were seen as the cause of the rise in the cost of living. For their part, economists at the time regarded wholesale price indices as the appropriate indicators of economic activity.

3 Eight Generations of the Price Index

Various methods of "data collection" (see Box 2.2) have succeeded each other over time, marking a gradual advance towards a price index that aspired to a form of exhaustiveness. Just like the extension of the range of goods and services covered by the basket, the extension of coverage to all households (and not just a household representative of the working class) was presented as statistical progress. All this was happening, it is true, in a period in which economic and social equality was still regarded by most of the actors concerned as an attainable goal.

Box 2.2 Data Collection

To speak of "collection" as if it were a matter of "harvesting" prices once they had "ripened" may give the impression that the exercise is a purely technical one (Piriou 1992). The price collectors working for national statistical offices are never in fact mere collectors. Their job, rather, is to interpret the facts that can be observed in the shops. They have to track a series of prices charged for products regarded as (strictly) identical from one month to the next. Now it may be that the current product is not in the shop at the time of the visit, that it may have been permanently delisted by the retailer in question, that it has been replaced by a product that may "appear" to be similar or even that it has been replaced by a product of a different "quality". It is then up to the price collector to assess whether "the differences in characteristics between the products would have justified a price difference in the base period". Moreover, as we shall see in the following chapters, the statistical practices adopted by the price collectors and national statistical offices influence the way in which prices are processed statistically. In the field, this applies particularly to differences in the interpretation of situations in which the boundaries between goods of variable quality are somewhat porous. Sometimes this variation in quality will be interpreted as a cosmetic change introduced for marketing purposes, in which case the price variation will be interpreted as a pure one. On other occasions, the variation in quality will be regarded as a genuine change in some of the good's substantive characteristics, in which case the variation in price will be reduced by a quality "discount". On yet other occasions, this variation in quality will be regarded as a radical change. In this last case, this variation in quality will be regarded as the introduction of a new good and will be interpreted not as a price increase but as a change in quality.

Between 1914 and 1949, the French National Statistics Office initially adopted a basket of 13 items, which gradually increased to 34 items, while INSEE defined a 'working-class family of four persons living in Paris' as representative of what at that time could be regarded as a typical budget. Various generations of the index followed (there were eight in all between 1913 and 2016, see Table 1.3), each bringing with it reforms relating to the reference population, geographic area or the statistical sources used to calculate the weightings. In 2016, all consumers (in town and cities with more than 2000 inhabitants) and 97% of consumption were covered by the CPI.

Certain debates rumble on, particularly at European level, for example about the method for including rents in the price index, since practices vary from one country to another and the question has for a long time been a sensitive one, particularly because rents account for a large proportion of household consumption. In France, the scope of the CPI is restricted to consumption and excludes investment. On this basis, only the rents paid by tenants, together with the prices of the goods and services purchased for the day-to-day maintenance of the accommodation, are included in the index. This convention excludes the costs of acquiring accommodation and the cost of the capital required (interest charged on mortgage loans). It diverges from the treatment of rents in the national accounts, where the 'fictitious rent' convention (estimated by the imputed rent method) is used for owner-occupiers, despite the fact that at the beginning of the new millennium this category accounted for 53% of all households. This treatment and the conventions that underpin it has a very significant impact on the share of the Housing item in the budget coefficients used in computing the CPI (Table 2.2).

4 1950–1970: A Price Index Policy?

The retail price index, as it was still called in France in the 1950s, has always been a sensitive issue for politicians. Standard budgets, which were the object of fierce negotiations, seem like harbingers of the price indices and political battles that were to follow.

4.1 Standard Budgets

The first studies of standard (or family) budgets date from 1907, when the General Statistics Office (the SGF, forerunner of INSEE) launched a survey of 800 working-class families in Paris (Touchelay 2003). This survey enabled the SGF to produce estimations of the purchasing power of these typical households. However, the negotiations on these standard budgets were restarted at the beginning of the 1950s.

The post-war period was, after all, marked by intense debates in France in a context in which the Cold War was in its very early stages, the French

Table 2.2 The eight 'generations' of the French CPI: 1914–2019

	Year of change/ implementation	*Designation*	*Reference population*	*Geographic coverage*	*Consumer basket*	*Weightings*
First generation	1914 1914–1949	13 then 34-item index Base year 1914, then 1938	Working-class family, four people (two children)	Paris	29 food items 4 heating items lighting 1 maintenance product	Typical budgets
Second generation	1949 1950–1956	213-item index	Blue/ white-collar family, four people	*Département de la Seine*	Food (excl. fresh products and alcohol) Manufactures (excl. consumer durables, petrol, medicines) Some services	Family budget survey
Third generation	1957 1957–1962	250-item index	Blue/ white-collar households, more than two persons	*Département de la Seine* + 17 regional capitals	Food (excl. alcohol) Manufactures except some durable goods 50% of services	Family budget survey
Fourth generation	1962 1963–1970	259-item index	Blue/ white-collar households, more than two persons	All towns with more than 2000 inhabitants	Food (excl. alcohol) Manufactures except some durable goods 60% of services	Family budget survey
Fifth generation	1970 then 1980 1971–1992	296-item index	Household whose head is blue/ white-collar workers	All towns with more than 2000 inhabitants	All food Manufactures 'approximately' 80% of services	Updated annually on the basis of national accounts

Sixth generation	1990–1993	265-item index Introduction of a new 'non-tobacco' index in 1992 (for indexation of the national minimum wage in particular)	All households	All towns with more than 2000 inhabitants	All food Manufactures 'Approximately' 85% of services (vets, funeral services, car hire, sea and coastal transport, ambulances, air travel (standard flight)) Rate of coverage of CPI: 88.3%	Updated annually on the basis of national accounts
Seventh generation	1998			The scope of the CPI becomes that of household actual final consumption (monetary transactions)	Rate of coverage of the CPI base 1998 94.1% New inclusions: insurance (car and house), social protection services (nurseries, child minder and retirement homes), housing-related services Use of the Coicop classification: Classification Of Individual Consumption by Purpose	
Eighth generation	2015 2016–	1100-variety index (product families)		99 towns and cities with more than 2000 inhabitants	Rate of coverage of 97% of all goods and services Eurostat Coicop classification adopted at a more detailed level than in 1998	

Source: based on Saglio (1993, p. 4) for the first six generations. Various INSEE methodological memoranda for the seventh and eighth

Communist Party had been excluded from the Ramadier government since 1947 and what some saw as social progress (beginning of the three post-war decades of economic growth) contrasted starkly with what others saw as the absolute impoverishment of Parisian manual workers compared with the pre-war period (Maurice Thorez). It was in this fraught context that a new wave of collective agreements was negotiated (the first dated from the 1920s), which also paved the way for the introduction of a minimum wage in France. The space in which these debates took place was a conference on 'costs, wages and remunerations' that provided an opportunity for the social partners to raise the question of the type of index that might be used to measure the cost of living. The trade unions drew up a number of standard budgets (for an unskilled worker in the Paris region) that were intended as a basis for determining what a basket that was representative of household budgets and of the evolution of its cost would contain. These exercises fed into the negotiations and provided the first points of reference for indexing wages to prices.

These debates of the 1950s were concomitant with those on the introduction of a minimum wage. They confirm that the standard budget approach preceded the intense struggles around the price index. A trade unionist reported that the negotiations between unions and employers on these questions were very bitter: "The employers", he said, "refused to include a suit in the standard budget because they said that manual workers wore one twice in their lives: once to get married and a second time to get buried. Well, that's the sort of relationship we had at the time with the employers' association in the metalworking and mining industries".

The national minimum wage was established by the 1950 Act and was regarded as a major policy measure in the revival of consumption and the fight against poverty. The bouts of inflation at the end of the 1940s and the period of calm at the beginning of the 1950s led to the introduction of mechanisms to regulate workers' income by indexing the minimum wage to the price index from 1952 onwards. This indexation amounted to the introduction of a sliding wage scale: if the price index increased by more than 5% (and by more than 2% in 1957), the minimum wage was automatically adjusted in order to maintain workers' purchasing power (Touchelay, op. cit.). This period in which the state sought to control industrial disputes through these mechanisms also saw the institutionalisation of the measurement of inflation. While they certainly ensured that purchasing power remained stable to some extent, these various forms of indexation also tended to shift the emphasis of some of the struggles to the *measurement* of the cost of living, which in turn placed questions of distribution at the very heart of the issues around measurement—with all the uncertainties inherent in this sense of the term (see Chaps. 5 and 7).

4.2 Wage Indexation Policies and Index Policies

The years between 1950 and 1970 clearly illustrate how the state exercised its power in order to bring inflation under control. Two indices coexisted at that time: one for Paris, the other for the French provinces. The indexation of wages, provided for in the 1952 Act, was based solely on the Paris price index (the 213-item index) and not the 183-item index used in the provinces.

In the years following the war, the 1947 International Conference of Labour Statisticians recommended that the price index should be transparent. "The index is based on the budget of a 4-person family of wage-earners of modest means in the *département* of the Seine" (Touchelay 2003, p. 7). The tensions around the index were an inherent part of this period, with the public authorities exerting direct pressure on the price of products wherever it could, particularly on administered prices "and on the prices of public services included in the composition of the index" (Touchelay 2014, p. 119). The power of the state to influence the index was made easier at the time because, at the beginning of 1950s, statisticians published all the goods included in the composition of the index out of a concern to ensure transparency. The Act of 18 July 1952 made INSEE's retail price index the cornerstone of the automatic indexation of the minimum wage (Touchelay 2003). As early as 1953, 'L.A.Vincent indicated that the government was trying to exert its influence on the items used to calculate the index'. Relations between INSEE and the General Directorate for Prices, which was tasked with enforcing the regulations, 'deterioriated'. "Faced with the sharp spike in inflation in the 1950s, governments did not hesitate to bring pressure to bear on the prices of the products included in INSEE's index" (Touchelay 2003, p. 12). Thus the General Directorate for Prices "sought to obtain the list of shops in which the prices of the constituent elements of the index were collected"; in the autumn of 1952, the Directorate General, supported by Antoine Pinay, President of the Council, "interceded with Francis-Louis Closon, requesting that he provides them with that list" (Touchelay 2003, p. 12). Things became more strained around the years 1955–1957, when a new base for the index was being constructed that introduced fruit and vegetables. The government suspected that their inclusion in the basket would have an inflationary effect on the index: "At the beginning of 1957, numerous deputies and senators from the rural and agricultural *départements* called for INSEE to give guarantees as to the effects of including fruits and vegetables in the index". This index was also disputed by trade unionists. Touchelay relates that one trade union proposed substituting a 170-item index, the so-called light blue-collar index for the 230-item index then in use. The INSEE index was criticised for "representing a standard of living higher than that of the light blue-collar index". The director of INSEE "then pointed out that the hypothetical income of the light blue-collar index was very poorly represented in Paris, since it equated virtually to that of the Algerian proletariat" (Touchelay 2003, p. 16).

In general terms, wage indexation, on the one hand, and government index policy, on the other, caused some companies to modify their commercial strategies. Béatrice Touchelay mentions this very characteristic example of the Berlitz school, which was enjoined by the government to reduce the price of private lessons since they were part of the price index basket. "The director spoke to INSEE, suggesting that this price should be replaced by that for group lessons, which workers of modest means were more likely to attend. The suggestion was accepted. The statisticians soon observed, however, that the school increased the price of private lessons considerably and began to offer semi-private lessons that were much more expensive than the group lessons" (Touchelay 2003, p. 13). The state, on the one hand, was striving for a form of statistical deflation by requiring the company to reduce its prices; the company, on the other hand, while complying with the request, was also nursing its profit margins by exercising its price-setting freedom in other services.

Nevertheless, given the state of power relations at the time, these struggles to increase purchasing power, on the one hand, and to bring inflation under control, on the other, led to a sharp increase in real wages, at the same time as very significant labour productivity gains were being achieved and, more generally, the wage-labour nexus was being increasingly socialised. The retrospective study carried out by Baudelot and Lebeaupin in 1979 showed that nominal wages increased tenfold over these three decades. For its part, INSEE puts the increases in purchasing power between 1960 and 1974 at 5.6% per year (Bournay and Pionnier 2007). Two phenomena serve to shed light on the increase in the minimum wage relative to the retail price index at the end of the 1960s (Fig. 2.1). The first is the policies pursued in the wake of the events of May 1968, which led to a spectacular uprating of the minimum wage, as well as to the change-over in 1970 from the SMIG (*salaire minimum interprofessionnel garanti*), which was uprated in line with inflation, to the SMIC (*salaire minimum interprofessionnel de* croissance), which was uprated in line not only with inflation but also with the increase in the average wage. The SMIC continues to be uprated in line with the evolution of the price index but the other wages are also taken into account "marking the recognition of a certain parity in the evolution of wages" (Boyer and Hollingsworth 1997).

4.3 A 'Traumatic' Period for INSEE

This period, which is sometimes interpreted as that in which control of the CPI was put into the hands of politicians, left a lasting mark on INSEE. This led the agency to compile, from the 1960s onwards, a secret list of varieties making up the CPI basket and in general to surround the composition of the CPI with a certain degree of confidentiality with a view to avoiding any direct political pressure on the index. It may be—and this is simply a hypothesis—that this traumatic period fostered the development of an increasingly autonomous space at some remove from a calm and confident engagement with the public debate and democracy on these questions of general concern. In any event, the policy of bringing the prices of index items under control gradually faded away from the mid-1960s onwards, even though inflation persisted and some state enterprises voiced criticisms of a situation in which they were unable to use the economic lever of price increase, following the example of the RATP, the state-owned Paris public transport operator. As we shall see, power relations were subsequently to follow other paths, particularly since INSEE was in organisational terms under the supervision of the Ministry of Economics and Finance.

4.4 A Different Story in the USA During the 1950s?

The sharp increase in inflation recorded during the 1950s and the indexation policies that followed in its wake were managed differently in the USA. Two economists, Ruggles at Yale and Rees at the University of Chicago, at a Joint Economic Committee in 1958, revisited the

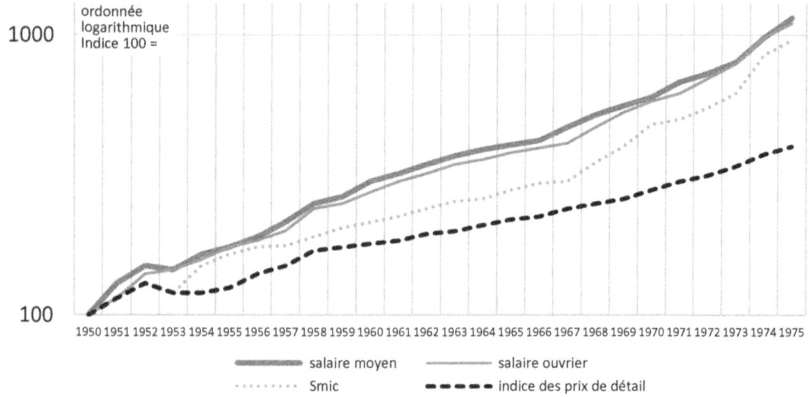

Fig. 2.1 Evolution of the average wage, of manual workers' wages, of the minimum wage and of retail prices from 1950 to 1975. (Source: Baudelot and Lebeaupin 1979)

arguments advanced to explain the rise in inflation. Rather than emphasising the trade unions' role or that of the industrial monopolies in the increase in inflation, Ruggles and Rees put forward a new hypothesis, namely that official statistics were incapable of "capturing a central form of growth in post-war economics, namely innovation as reflected in the quality of products and of new products" (Ruggles and Rees 1959). These were the first political episodes in an investigation into the difficulty of using statistical price measurement to capture quality effects and the first recommendations made by economists with a view to improving the method of measurement used in computing price indices. While the objective of this committee was to take better account of the introduction of new products and of variations in quality and productivity, the technical changes proposed led almost as a matter of course to a slowdown in the general increase in prices and therefore militated against redistribution. Stapleford shows that the NBER recruited George Stigler from the University of Chicago during this period; it was at his suggestion that the notion of analysing 'cost of living indices on the basis of constant utility' was included in the American statistical manual, which was a very standard or very utilitarian way of measuring a constant-quality cost of living. As early as 1959, the report recommended that the CPI should become a constant utility or well-being index and that an index of this kind would have recorded lower price increases since the Second World War than those recorded by the official consumer price index. Among the statistical innovations, particular mention should be made of the use of geometric means in establishing certain micro price indices based on heterogeneous varieties that sought to take account of the possible (rational) tendency of consumers to substitute certain products with lower priced equivalents. The use of such a mean also leads *automatically* to a reduction in the price increase. Also of note are the first proposals for calculating the quality effect. These proposals generally operated statistically as a discount on the evolution of the price in question. The general idea was that if the good improves over time, the increase in its price may reflect an increase in quality rather than in the pure price (see Chap. 1). From this point of view, this discount is explained by an increase in the functionalities and power of certain products (cars, computers, etc.) and by the possibility of acquiring an increasingly diversified range of increasingly durable and reliable goods.

Ideas did not yet flow freely across national borders in the 1950s and Europe remained relatively aloof from this debate until the end of the 1970s. In the USA, however, the indexation of earnings and pressure from mainstream economists led little by little to a situation in which it appeared evident that the price index would gradually have to edge its way towards a cost of living index, in accordance with the definition of such an index offered by neoclassical economists, namely that it was a measure of the variation in the expenditure required in order to obtain the same level of utility, or welfare. Most of these recommendations were spectacularly corrected 20 years later by the Boskin Boskin (1996) (see Chap. 4), which attracted considerable media attention.

5 The Life of the CGT Index (1972–1998)

The effects of wage indexation and social security benefits (and of tax bands) on political sensitivities about the price index displaced some of the political struggles to the field of statistics involved in measuring the cost of living, with all the vagueness inherent in that term. While the initial tensions around the price index date in France from the 1950s, when governments were exerting direct pressure on the prices of the goods and services used to compute the index, they took a more directly confrontational turn at the beginning of the 1970s with the construction and publication of an index by the powerful CGT trade union.

5.1 *The Origins of the CGT Index*

After two decades of stand-offs between state and trade unions around the measurement of inflation and the drafting of standard budgets, the CGT declared itself extremely dissatisfied because, in its view, the index significantly underestimated the increase in the cost of living (defined at that time as the expenditure required to live), particularly for manual workers. However, the major crisis of confidence that found expression in the production by the CGT of a counter-index from 1972 onwards cannot be dissociated either from a challenge to what was to emerge as an initial phase of financial globalisation, when the USA, followed by the rest of the Western world, abandoned the gold standard in 1971, turning the capitalist world into a world of self-referential and competing currencies and, above all, opening the door to financial speculation (Théret 2010).

While it was the CGT's index that drew most of the attention, largely because of the confederation's important position in the French trade union landscape of the time, most of the trade unions were involved. The negotiations on the standard budgets had, after all, led the main trade unions and other voluntary associations to propose their own price indices. Thus as early as the 1950s, the CFDT had constructed a price index on the basis of a four-person family of modest means and the INSEE price survey; the FO tracked the evolution of the standard budget of a single unskilled worker calculated on the basis of the INSEE price survey; the National Union of Familial Associations (UNAF) computed a standard budget for a four-person family with two children aged 6 and 12. And the CNAPF, for its part, also tracked a standard budget for a family with two children aged 6 and 12 headed by a steelworker in the Paris region.

For its part, having measured the evolution of prices each quarter by means of a standard budget compiled by the Higher Commission for Collective Agreements, the CGT concluded that the time had come to construct a better designed monthly index and to do so independently. In 1970, the CGT's executive committee commissioned a price index from its experts. This initiative was facilitated greatly by the very high level of trade union membership in all departments of INSEE at the time and by the close partnership that existed then between the CGT and the CFDT. Trade unionists at INSEE actively supported the CGT in its efforts to produce statistics without the agreement of the general management. A statistics manual for the use of negotiators was compiled and circulated among the advocates of this counter-index.

5.2 *The Specific Characteristics of the CGT Index*

The first version of the CGT index was presented in issue 888 of *Le Peuple* on 15 March 1972. The unique characteristic of the CGT index was that it was a consumer price index for a four-person family (two children aged 10 and 15), tenants, headed by a skilled manual worker living in the Paris region. The CGT undertook its own price survey with the aim of producing something that looked like the INSEE price index but without having the resources to do so. The CGT relied on students, supervised by trade unionists, who were sufficiently persuaded of the cause to complete the price survey in the Paris region each month. The index was computed by the central purchasing cooperative of the mining regions, a CGT cooperative, which made available the necessary computing resources.

The first weighting by major items in the CGT index allocated 36.0% to food, 8.9% to clothes and 27.8% to housing (see Table 2.3).

The composition of the CGT's price index took the idea of the Laspeyres index to the letter. It was based on a fixed basket of goods; consequently, no discount was applied (e.g. to the nominal price increase) in order to take account of any increase in quality. The arguments put forward by the CGT concerned the issue of monopolistic supernormal profits, advertising and waste as well the idea that 'it is not because a model is more expensive that it is of better quality' and the constraining nature of some changes in quality. If the lower quality item were no longer on sale, whether it be an

Table 2.3 Weighting by major item, CGT index, 1972

Item	*Weight in the index (in %)*
Food	36.0
Clothing	8.9
Housing	27.8
Of which: rent and charges	*16.8*
Others	*11.0*
Personal hygiene, health	7.6
Transport, telecommunications	9.7
Cultural and leisure activities	6.7
Miscellaneous	3.3
Total	100.0

Source: *Le Peuple*, issue 888, 1972

item of clothing or a car, consumers might be forced, despite themselves, to purchase the item of higher quality. This issue, which was illustrated in the 1970s by examples of clothes, was later to be a particularly acute one with the rapid spread of information technologies in the world of consumption. These technologies change rapidly and their functionalities increase tenfold, but the old models quickly become unavailable, forcing households to purchase the new items.

The decisions not to take the quality effect into account, to increase greatly the weight of housing in the index (in 1971, housing had a weighting coefficient of 4.7% in the official index, while rents had a coefficient of more than 16% in the CGT index) and not to take seasonal variations into account (which in the price index of the time were amortised over 12 months) meant that the CGT index was permanently 2 to 4 points higher than the INSEE index. This is what is indicated by the two graphs reconstructed from data from the monthly magazine *Le Peuple*, in which the data used to compute the CGT price index were set out in a full-page table (Figs. 2.2 and 2.3).

It should be noted that, if the CPI was 2 to 4 points higher than the official index, it should have been inferred that economic growth was also

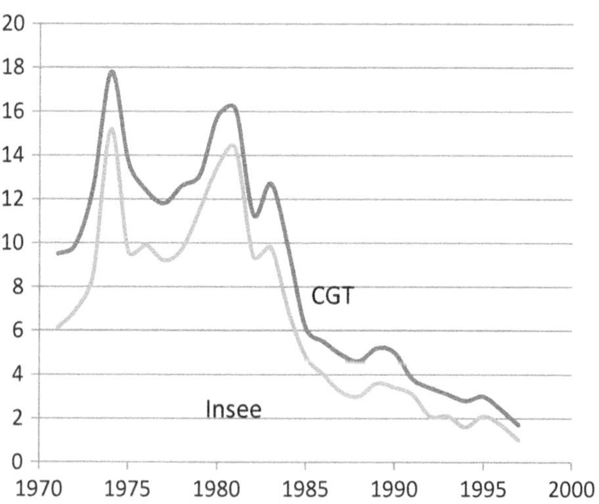

Fig. 2.2 Comparison of the annual rate of growth of the CPI and of the CGT index: 1972–1998. (Source: Data taken from the monthly magazine *Le Peuple*: 1972–1998. CGT archives, Montreuil)

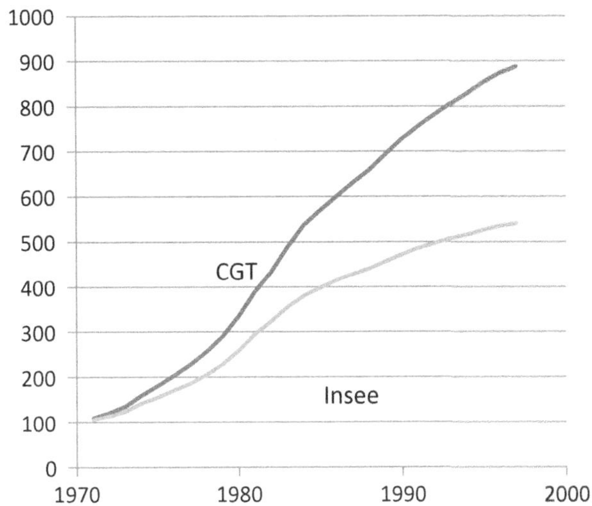

Fig. 2.3 Comparison of the evolution of the CPI and of the CGT index, base 100 in 1971. (Source: Data taken from the monthly magazine *Le Peuple*: 1972–1998. CGT archives, Montreuil)

being overestimated by about 2 to 4 points per year, since consumption is the central component of GDP.

In any event, the CGT index played an important role in industrial relations until the beginning of the 1980s (Piriou 1992, p. 82). Trade unionists who were active at the time relate how this alternative indicator served as a real bargaining lever. While few companies relied on it directly to negotiate wage increases, the trade unions, in contrast, adopted a cross between the official index and the CGT index, particularly in those industries in which the CGT was particularly well established, such as the chemical and metalworking industries. The nationwide debate that the CGT triggered by publishing its index every month functioned like a veritable resonance chamber in the power struggle between unions and employers. "It was a rare event", said a former trade unionist in charge of the index, "when there wasn't one, two, even three leaflets on the price index, the cost of living index, INSEE's endeavours, the fact that the bosses didn't want to abandon the official index. It had become the bosses' index… That's what INSEE couldn't bear". The trade union, as we can see, communicated with its alternative price index, as if it were a cost of living index (see Box 2.3)

Box 2.3 'Inflation', 'Cost of Living' and 'Purchasing Power'

The cost of living and purchasing power

The cost of living is, on the face of it, a layman's term, one that can be easily appropriated by any individual or consumer. A socioeconomic history of the measurement of inflation shows that, from the 1950s to the 1970s, economists and politicians used the two notions of 'cost of living' and 'inflation' imprecisely. Thus the literature is full of references to 'rise in the cost of living' when what is actually meant is 'rise in inflation'. Common sense would suggest that the cost of 'my' life rises if what it costs me to live rises. The cost of 'my' life may rise, all other things being equal in terms of income. In this sense, therefore, the cost of living is, on the face of it, separate from income, which leaves a gulf between the notion of 'cost of living' and that of 'purchasing power'. Purchasing power is, after all, clearly defined as the quantity of goods and services that can be purchased with the income at one's disposal and is thus dependent on the evolution of the general level of prices, on the one hand, and the evolution of income, on the other.

The cost of living and normativity

The cost of living may be normative in character, as the economic literature suggests, but it may also be understood relatively independently of any normative characteristics. After all, in seeking to measure the cost of 'my' life, my aim is not to ascertain what I need in order to enjoy a predetermined standard of living but rather to calculate the cost (and the changes in the cost) of that which is available to me. Thus it would not be illogical to take the view that the cost of living is close to the cost of household expenditures. Furthermore, this approach to the cost of living based on the cost of average household expenditure is the concept closest to the approach adopted by national accounts, which is based on a final consumer price index.

These intuitive deliberations around a 'cost of living' index are far removed from a price index that aims to calculate the evolution of the expenditure required to purchase a fixed basket of consumer goods and services.

They are also equally far removed from a constant utility index, which is designed to measure the minimum expenditures required to maintain a certain level of 'well-being', the notion of well-being being itself normative and the object of a multiplicity of debates in the socioeconomic literature. These debates are concerned as much with its various theoretical foundations as with the methods of measuring it, the two being closely linked.

5.3 *Competitive Devaluation and the End of the CGT Index*

The tensions around the production of this CGT index intensified throughout the 1980s, at the same time as interest in price indices was waning. The de-indexation of wages at the beginning of the 1980s, in an attempt to subdue inflationary expectations, changed the context considerably. In fact, a new method of wage setting was replacing this policy; from now on, wages were indexed to a 'forecast inflation rate' that served as a point of reference for wage increases. The innovation was that 'ex post indexation to a past inflation rate was replaced by ex ante indexation to a moderate forecast inflation rate'; this new approach to indexation was accompanied by a 'catch-up clause' that would come into force if the forecast rate diverged from the actual inflation rate recorded ex post (Bezbakh 2011, p. 95). Economists' forecasts always turned out in fact to be lower than the actual inflation rate (Chauvin and Le Bihan 2007) and helped to rein in increases in real wages from the beginning of the 1980s onwards.

At the same time as these changes in the context were taking place, trade unionists in the CGT confederation could not fail to notice that the fixed nature of the basket of goods used to compute the CGT price index was proving to be statistically unsustainable because of far-reaching changes in the modes of production and consumption that had taken place between 1970 and 1980, the years during which the CGT index was computed. As a result, the CGT's reference basket was facing a number of challenges: many of the products it contained had to be changed (e.g. because the goods whose prices were being collected were not on the shelves at the time of the survey, whether because of a failure of stock management, the disappearance of seasonal products or a product reaching the end of its life cycle) and the many innovations and the increase in the variety of products purchased had also to be taken into account.

And on the technical level as well, the changes in consumption meant that the fixed-basket CGT index increasingly failed to reflect those changes. Finally, as the graph below shows, the gap between the CGT index and the INSEE price index diminished over time, eventually becoming insignificant, reflecting the changes in the method used to compute the CGT index (Fig. 2.4).

Overall, the radical changes in economic policy, the introduction from the end of the 1970s onwards of monetarist policies aimed at controlling inflation, the increasing financialisation of the economy, as well as mass

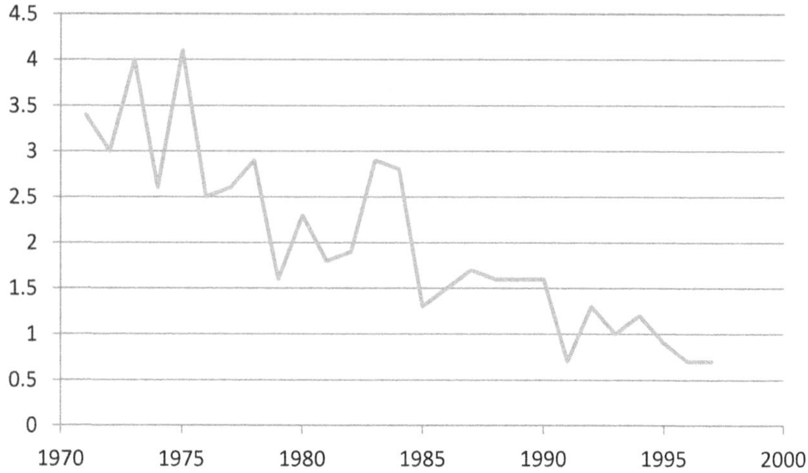

Fig. 2.4 Annual gap between the CGT price index and the INSEE CPI: 1972–1997 (in percentage points). (Source: data taken from the monthly magazine *Le Peuple*: 1972–1998. CGT Archives, Montreuil)

unemployment, the flexibilisation of work systems and the deterioration in working and employment conditions gradually diverted the trade unions' attention away from the CPI and how to measure it towards these new economic and political. As a result of all of this, the CGT stopped published its index in 1998. Nevertheless, like the preceding period in which the state had left its imprint on index policy, this period of turbulent relations between the CGT and INSEE left lasting marks on INSEE's subsequent behaviour which, at least until the 2010s, had become very sensitive to polemics and controversies around estimates of inflation while at the same time retaining a certain degree of freedom to decide how it should be estimated.

6 The 1990s and 2000s: Between Finance and Governmentality

6.1 *The Indexation of Financial Products*

Although wages had been partly de-indexed, other items were indexed for the first time during this period and those that followed. The indexation of financial products, which can be interpreted as an innovation introduced by the financialised state, reinvigorated the fevered debate around the calculation of the price index. This was the major turning point in economic policy at the beginning of the 1980s. Debt was increasingly being seen as an investment, which in turn required inflation to be tamed in order to guarantee the returns to savers and creditors alike (Lemoine 2016). In order to reassure and protect savers even more, arrangements for indexing financial products were introduced from the beginning of the 1990s (Tinel 2016, p. 50). In 1997, a mechanism known as TIPS (Treasury Inflation Protected Securities) was put in place in order to provide investors with a constant financial return regardless of the rate of inflation (Greenlees and McClelland 2008, p. 4). A year after this measure had been put in place in the USA, the French Treasury, the *Trésor public*, placed around 10% of its debt in the form of OATs (*obligations assimilables du Trésor*), which are government bonds issued with maturities of 7–50 years and indexed to the price index excluding tobacco (OATi) or to the HICP (OATie). These instruments, sometimes known as 'DSK Bonds' (Lemoine 2016, p. 145), were introduced by the finance minister of the time, Dominique Strauss-Kahn, and effectively index the interest rate to the inflation rate in order to protect creditors from inflationary risks. These creditors, for example pension funds, often have to pay out flows of money that are indexed to inflation (pensions, annuities, regulated savings accounts, etc.). Thus they are protected from these inflationary risks by these OATi bonds, which they often purchase, it is true, at yields lower than the fixed rates but adjusted for the inflation rate, which enables them to recoup their outlay.

Invited to comment on a report compiled on behalf of the Council for Economic Analysis and entitled *Mesurer le pouvoir d'achat/Measuring purchasing power* (Moati and Rochefort 2008), in which the authors argue for a plurality of prices indices, Jacques Delpa, then an economist at BNP-Paribas, highlighted the decisive role of DSK bonds in consolidating financialisation. He put the amount of public debt indexed against the CPI at 150 billion euros in 2008 and declared, with regard to the controversies surrounding the calculation of the CPI: "If the current fault-finding were to continue and call into question the integrity of the CPI, if investors came to believe that the CPI seriously underestimates inflation in France, then there is a serious risk that they will sell their bonds or that, in order to remain invested in OATi or CADESi bonds, they will demand that they linked to an index showing a much higher rate of inflation. This would be a terrible blow to the public finances, to France's financial credibility and to the debt issue programme based on bonds indexed to prices. Until now, the debate on the CPI has not been regarded as serious by investors. But if this were to be the case, how could the Treasury and the CADES (Caisse d'Amortissement de la Dette Sociale) continue their programme of funding the OATi and CADESi bonds?" To conclude, he wrote: "This is why the government, and in particular the Ministry of Finance, should act quickly to put an end to this polemic on the French CPI and not create several general price indices, otherwise there is a risk that ten years of Treasury credibility in the bond markets will be severely dented" (Delpla 2008, p. 166). The frenzy was at its height, and the bankers were getting involved in the debate.

6.2 *A Price Index 'Without Tobacco'*

At the beginning of the 1990s, INSEE ran into another controversy when the government proposed constructing an index that excluded tobacco products. Tobacco was, after all, regularly targeted by public policies, particularly through a tax regime that had become gradually tougher in order to encourage a reduction in its consumption. Increases in the price to consumers were impacting on the general CPI. After much heated disagreement and debate, two indices were finally adopted, one with tobacco for international comparisons and for uses relating to European convergence (see below) and the other without tobacco for indexation purposes. This decision was initially incorporated into the act of January 1990 on measures relating to social security and health, article 51 of which stipulated that "the National Institute of Statistics and Economic Studies has an obligation to publish each month a CPI from which all references to the price of tobacco are excluded". The Neiertz Act on the fight against smoking, nicotine addiction and alcoholism, which was promulgated a year later, is typical of the various disputes that continually stoked the debates. On the one hand, eliminating tobacco from the index obviously enabled government to increase the taxation of this mass consumption item without any impact on the price and neither, therefore, directly on wages. This was also a way of sorting out the more or less 'pure' and more or less legitimate prices that would make up the basket. On the one hand, the price of tobacco, an administered price, had been legally removed from the basket. On the other hand, the other prices, interpreted as 'true' consumer prices, were included in the basket. This exclusion of the price of tobacco was also a way of introducing a form of morality into public action measures; as a result, statistics emerged as a veritable instrument of government, here aimed explicitly at normalising consumer behaviour.

Thus much against INSEE's wishes, the tobacco episode, and the production of these two indices, opened up the Pandora's box of multiple price indices that were to be constructed differently depending on the uses to which they were to be put.

References

Armatte, M. 2005. « Lucien March (1859-1933). Une statistique mathématique sans probabilité ? » *Journ@l Electronique d'Histoire des Probabilités et de la Statistique*, vol 1, n°1, p. 1–19.

Baudelot, Ch., and A. Lebeaupin. 1979. Les salaires entre 1950 et 1975. *Économie et Statistique*, juillet-août, n° 113: 15–22.

Bezbakh, P. 2011. *Inflation et désinflation*. Paris: La Découverte, coll. « Repères ».

Boskin, M.J., E. Dulberger, R. Gordon, Z. Griliches, and D. Jorgenson. 1996. *Toward a More Accurate Measure of the Cost of Living*. Final Report to the Senate Finance Committee, December 4.

Bournay, J., and P.-A. Pionnier. 2007. L'économie française: ruptures et continuités de 1959 à 2006. *Insee Première*, n° 1136, mai.

Boyer, R., and J.-R. Hollingsworth. 1997. *Contemporary Capitalism: The Embeddedness of Institutions*. Cambridge University Press.

Chauvin, V., and H. Le Bihan. 2007. Mesures et perception de l'inflation en France et dans la zone euro. État des lieux. *Bulletin de la Banque de France*, n° 160, avril, pp. 19–35.

Chélini, M.-P. 1998. *Inflation, État et opinion en France de 1944 à 1952*. Comité pour l'histoire économique et financière de la France, coll. « Études générales ».

Delpla, J. 2008. Commentaire. In *Mesurer le pouvoir d'achat*, Ph. Moati et R. Rochefort, 163–168.

Greenlees, J., and R. McClelland. 2008. Addressing Misconceptions about the Consumer Price Index. *Monthly Labour Review*, August, pp. 1–19.

Lemoine, B. 2016. *L'ordre de la dette*. Paris: La Découverte.

March, L. 1911. Salaires et coût de l'existence à diverses époques, jusqu'en 1910. SGF Paris.

Moati, Ph., and R. Rochefort. 2008. *Mesurer le pouvoir d'achat, Rapport pour le CAE*. Paris: La Documentation française.

Moden, J. 1982. L'indice des prix à la consommation. *Courrier hebdomadaire du CRISP* 978–979 (33): 1–38.

Piriou, J.-P. 1992. *L'indice des prix*. 2e rééd. Paris: La Découverte, coll. « Repères ».

Rouchet, J. 2016. D'une crise à l'autre. 1907 et la naissance du suivi de la conjoncture à la SGF. colloque des 70 ans de l'Insee, Paris, mai.

Ruggles, R., and A. Rees. 1959. US Congress, Joint Economic Committee. *Staff Report on Employment Growth, and Price Levels*, 86th Congress, 1st sess. December 24, 1959, 109.

Saglio, J. 1993. Le nouvel indice des prix à la consommation. *Économie et Statistique*, n° 267, 1, pp. 3–12.

Stapleford Th, A. 2009. *The Cost of Living in America. A Political History of Economic Statistics 1880–2000.* Cambridge: Cambridge University Press.

Théret, B. 2010. L'argent public et les régimes économiques de l'ordre politique. Entretien avec Bruno Théret. Vincent Gayon et Benjamin Lemoine, 2010/3, *Genèses*, pp. 136–152.

Tinel, B. 2016. *Dette publique: sortir du catastrophisme.* Paris: Raisons d'agir.

Touchelay, B. 2003. Cinquante ans d'indice des prix de détail en France, des 13 aux 250 articles: un apprentissage scientifique et politique. communication au colloque Histoire et gestion, CRG, IAE, Toulouse: « Mesure(s) », novembre.

———. 2014. Les ordres de la mesure des prix. Luttes politiques, bureaucratiques et sociales autour de l'indice des prix à la consommation (1911–2012). *Politix*, 2014/1, n° 105: 117–138.

CHAPTER 3

The European Turning Point

1 Maastricht (1992) and the HICP

The 1992 Maastricht Treaty, which established the European Union (EU) and set out a timeline for the creation and implementation of the Economic and Monetary Union (EMU), laid down the convergence criteria that the countries interested in joining the EMU would have to meet before and after integration. In particular, the public deficit was to be maintained below 3% of GDP and the public debt below 60% of GDP.

1.1 Maastricht and Inflation

These criteria are also anti-inflationary, since with regard to interest rates and inflation the Treaty stipulates that the inflation rate must not be more than 1.5 percentage points greater than that of the three member states that are the best performers in terms of price stability. Thus from the end of the 1980s onwards, those countries seeking membership of the EMU prepared to put in place rigorous policies that would meet the European criteria, facilitate greater coordination of the methods used to measure inflation and, more generally, institute a form of "automatic government" (Savage 2005). Even though procedures for harmonising the measurement of inflation were introduced at global level as early as 1925 (on the occasion of the second international conference of labour statisticians convened by the governing body of the International Labour Office, ILO

F. Jany-Catrice, *A Political Economy of the Measurement of Inflation*,
https://doi.org/10.1007/978-3-030-59940-9_3

et al. 2004), this coordination became an imperative coordinated by Eurostat. Attempting what seemed to be an impossible task, since the countries had very disparate statistical systems, from October 1995 the European Union adopted a framework regulation that laid the foundations for a harmonised methodology to be used by the member states in constructing consumer price indices. Production and publication of the HICP are mandatory. It must cover 'the same consumer goods and services and use the same classification', namely the COICOP (Classification of Individual Consumption by Purpose).

Through a succession of regulations and directives with the force of law, the European Statistical Office (Eurostat) became established as the authoritative body in the harmonisation of the definitions, classifications, methods and scope of the price indices in the countries of the EMU. The HICP was adopted by the European Central Bank as the indicator of price stability. However, the HICP and the consumer price indices in the various member states are calculated differently.

The Maastricht criteria, on the one hand, and the following phase during which individual countries prepared to qualify for membership of the European monetary union, on the other, gradually removed inflation from the sphere of economic policy. Inflation was, after all, one of the possible means of reducing the debt-to-GDP ratio, as the economies of the period between 1950 and 1980 tried to do. According to the economist Bruno Tinel, this constraining of economies henceforth characterised by very low inflation marked the 'triumph' of the financial lenders, since inflation made it possible to alter "the distribution of income between lenders

Box 3.1 The COICOP Classification

The COICOP classification is a functionalist representation of the goods and services consumed. Since 2016, the COICOP has comprised four internationally standardised levels (only three levels from 1998 to 2016): level 1 is broken down into a number of divisions (e.g.: 'clothing and shoes'), level 2 into 37 'groups' (e.g.: 'clothing'), level 3 into 95 'classes' (e.g.: 'clothing fabrics', 'clothes'), level 4 into 161 'sub-classes' (e.g.: 'women's underwear') and level 5 into 305 'items' (e.g.: 'skirt', 'dress', 'women's trousers').

The most detailed level is made up of 'varieties', a variety being composed of the price of a good *i* sold at sales outlet *j*.

and borrowers" (Tinel 2016, p. 49). From an economic point of view, since inflation could no longer absorb part of the public debt, welfare states were increasingly encouraged to reduce the scope of their activities by desocialising a significant share of expenditure and hence of consumption. The increasingly technical nature and objectivation of economic policy choices in debt instruments and institutions adopting a purely technical approach in order to keep the inflation rate low, all beyond the reach of democratic bodies, also caused member states to lose some of their sovereignty.

1.2 The HICP

1.2.1 The Context in Which the HICP Was Created

The plan for the establishment of the European Union and the European Central Bank provided for the creation of an index that would be used as a key criterion of convergence in the measurement of price stability. Thus according to Eurostat's website, the HICP was designed in such a way as "to provide the measure of the increase in consumer prices within the European Union and eurozone" that best lent itself "to evaluating the degree of convergence and of price stability within the framework of analyses of monetary policy".

France implemented this new classification from 1998 onwards at the time of the transition to a seventh-generation price index. It is not without interest to note that whereas the four preceding decades (1950–1990) had been marked by political struggles between the state and INSEE (1950–1970) or between the trade unions and INSEE (1970–1990) around the composition and estimation of the CPI, all the methodological regulations associated the HICP were henceforth binding on the country. Reliability and comparability were regarded as priorities and led to Eurostat assuming the role of controller and auditor of national statistics. Eurostat has continued to carry out regular audits in the national statistics agencies, particularly since 2005, when a European code of good statistical practices was adopted that the national agencies were invited to follow. INSEE's practices have been audited twice, once in 2007 and again in 2015.

1.2.2 The HICP: The Calculation Principle

The HICP is a Laspeyres-type index. It is based, therefore, on households' consumption patterns and the composition of the consumer population in the base year. International organisations regard it as a pure price index "that measures the average variation in prices on the basis of the changed expenditure of maintaining the consumption pattern of households" (ILO et al. 2004, Annexe 1, p. 454). The principle of the HICP is that its coverage is household final monetary consumption. This definition has certain consequences. As in France, this definition means that, to date, the cost of buying property has not been included in the HICP (which is regarded in accounting terms as an act of investment by households). Similarly, the EU excludes owner-occupiers' imputed expenses (the 'imputed rent'), even though a plan to add an index of the net cost of acquisition for owner-occupiers to the HICP remains on Eurostat's files. If it were to be adopted in future, such an option would lead to a break with the economic principle that stipulates that the CPI is limited to consumer prices, with the index being gradually adjusted to the morphology of a GDP price deflator.

Because of the variable share of owner-occupier households, this methodological choice by the EU means that housing is weighted differently in the HICP from one member state to another. According to an already old study conducted by the Banque de France in 2003 (*Bulletin de la Banque de France*, no. 115, July 2003), the share of owner-occupiers was 53.1% and the share of housing costs (i.e. rents) in the HICP was 7.9%. In Germany, on the other hand, where the share of owner-occupiers was 41.0%, the share of housing costs in the HICP was 12.4%. Thus there are not inconsiderable differences that have effects on the general measure of the evolution of prices.

This option also leads to differentiated treatment for prices regulated, for example, by social policies. Thus in the case of the prices of certain public services, Eurostat takes account of net prices, as is the case notably in Germany, while the French CPI uses gross prices. In the case of medical services (e.g. the services provided by doctor and dentists, lab analyses, pharmaceuticals, etc.) and social services (health insurance, supplementary health insurance, day care, etc.), it is 'gross prices' that are used in calculating the French CPI, that is the market prices that would apply 'in the absence of social policy', while Eurostat opts for 'net prices' *after* deduction of social transfers in kind. The net price is the price that is actually—one might say monetarily—paid by consumers "after all or part of the cost has been paid by a social security agency or, more generally, by a government or state agency" (Barret et al. 2003). While these choices may result in different price levels, changes in public policy, in social security reimbursements, for example, can have marked effects on the variation in one or other of the prices depending on the convention adopted. According to certain commentators, "monitoring the price of healthcare would make the index dependent on government decisions, thereby blurring measurement of the pure inflationary process in the economy" (Barret et al. 2003, p. 5), which is what the CPI is supposed to capture. Boskin voiced a similar criticism of the USA in 1996. Barret et al., for example, show that "in July 2000 the annual variation in healthcare prices was 1.4% according to the HICP but only 0.3% according to the CPI". This had direct repercussions on the overall index, since the HICP for that year was 0.3 points higher than the CPI. And the case of the UK even suggests that the difference in the inflation rate between the CPI and HICP was as high as 4 percentage points over the period between 1999 and 2002 (Barret et al., op. cit., p. 6).

2 The Price Index During the Changeover to the Euro

The changeover to the euro became a reality for the financial markets in 1999 and for consumers from 1 January 2002 with the introduction of a European fiduciary money. Whereas market confidence in this new currency seemed relatively assured, governments and the European Union itself went to great lengths to establish trust between citizens and the euro, putting forward several arguments, among which was the low inflation rate of the 1990s. The French minister of the economy, Laurent Fabius, wrote an opinion piece in *Le Monde* on the day the euro officially became legal tender in which he insisted that the currency would be more stable in future than the franc, which had been devalued '20 times' over the last 50 years. "At less than 2%, inflation in the Eurozone is now permanently under control, ensuring that our currency will have a high level of domestic purchasing power" (*Le Monde*, 1st January 2002). Consumers were equipped with calculators so that they could do the impossible sums required to convert francs into euros, the exchange rate being 6.55957 francs to 1 euro.

The process of bringing the currency under control was regulated. In order to ease the changeover to the euro, the European Union signed an agreement with the leading retailers that included a 'commitment to maintain overall price stability between 1 November 2001 and 31 March

2002'. This commitment was implemented in France 'by means of national agreements (excluding agricultural, seasonal and variably priced products) between representatives of the food industry and the large-scale retailers', with inspectors from the Directorate General for Competition, Consumer Affairs and Fraud Control (DGCCRF) deployed to confirm any possible 'unexpected rises' (*Monde*, 11 January 2002).

There was great anxiety in 2002 about a possible return of inflation (as early as January 11, *Le Monde* was asking: "Is the introduction of the euro going to reignite inflation?"), despite regular announcements that sought to quieten public opinion down. Suspicion fell by turns on the behaviour of small shopkeepers, cafés and restaurants and then the large retailers. In May 2002, the ECB was concerned about a sharp rise in prices in the service sector (28/05/2002, *Le Monde*). Consumer associations made their voices heard, highlighting the sharp increases in the prices of certain products (including oil and chocolate) (*UFC*, January 2003). Although the introduction of the euro was regarded as a major event, INSEE, in its quarterly report, took the view that its impact on inflation was negligible, of the order of 0.14 points of total inflation from January to September 2002. At the end of 2002, in an economic outlook report, INSEE recorded a relatively low rate of inflation: 2.2% for the year to the end of November 2002, compared with 1.7% in 2001, and further noted that the official consumer price index had met the Maastricht criteria.

2.1 *INSEE and the Changeover to the Euro*

Nevertheless, the changeover to the euro forced INSEE to put itself on a war footing during 2002, driven to do so by a press department overwhelmed with frequent enquiries from television, radio and newspaper journalists. The media suspected that the CPI was not taking account of all the changes in prices. INSEE responded to this in various ways, guardedly at first, as this data producing organisation has traditionally done in order to illuminate the public debate and not to anticipate it. The responses were provided by the prices division or by the economic trends department (*service conjuncture*), which was also drafted in to respond to media enquiries.

Faced with the public's firm belief ('public opinion' has been a term much bandied about since this time) that prices had increased sharply, INSEE demonstrated its educational skills: while it clung to the idea that inflation was very much under control, it gradually acknowledged over the course of the 2000s that there was indeed a plausible gap between the official index and individuals' perception of inflation. The National Council for Statistical Information (CNIS) devoted its annual meeting on 7 November 2005 to identifying the factors that might possibly explain this gap between perceptions of inflation and the CPI. It gave rise to a publication in the *CNIS-Chroniques* series, which appeared in March 2006 (no. 4, March 'De la perception à la mesure du pouvoir d'achat'). This publication focused first of all on the question of incomes, acknowledged "the disruption caused by the changeover to the euro" and proposed larger price increases for those with low incomes (p. 3).

The idea of a gap between individuals' perception of inflation and the official inflation rate gave rise to a multitude of reports, memoranda and working groups. In 2003, the IMF, whose managing director at the time was the German Horst Köhler, set up a working group on macroeconomic statistics and the CPI (Quinet 2008, p. 7). The IMF was undoubtedly being pressed hard by the European countries, notably Germany, which had faced this issue with a vengeance between 2001 and 2004. In France, two reports, one by the CNIS (*De la perception à la mesure du pouvoir d'achat*, 2006), the other by the Parliament (Mariton, *Mesurer pour comprendre*, 2008), reflected the increasingly fevered debate on the issue.

However, two reports attracted attention. The first was written by Philippe Moati and Robert Rochefort and submitted to the Council for Economic Analysis (*Conseil d'analyse économique*/CAE) in 2008 (Moati and Rochefort 2008). Rochefort was at the time a member of the CAE and was also director general of CRÉDOC (*Centre de recherche pour l'étude et l'observation des conditions de vie*). This report, which was particularly carefully compiled, had been commissioned by Dominique de Villepin, the then prime minister. A few months later, a commission on household purchasing power, chaired by Alain Quinet, was appointed by Christine Lagarde, the then finance minister. The commission sat for three months, bringing together "representatives of consumer and family associations, academic experts and experts from INSEE's economic and financial departments" (Quinet 2008). It drew to a large extent on the proposals contained in the Moati/Rochefort report for the CAE, "on the experience of the associations and on current research" (op. cit.).

The primary purpose of these various reports and working groups was to measure purchasing power and/or the CPI. All of them highlighted assessments of public opinion, and in particular public perceptions of inflation that diverged from the official measure of the price index. They provided an opportunity to outline some of the factors that might explain this divergence, which was persisting in France. The explanations offered (see below) convinced those among the social partners who were not contesting INSEE's work. Most of these reports argued that what was needed was to provide the public with better information on the price index. In particular, they noted that a positive inflation rate did not necessarily signify a direct loss of purchasing power, since purchasing power depends also on the evolution of nominal wages. However, some consumer organisations were irritated by the suggestion that all the public needed was to be better informed, since it necessarily implied that the large mass of the French population was simply ignorant.

2.2 *Advances in Measuring Perceptions of Inflation*

With the arrival of the euro in 2002, confidence in the new currency started to crumble in French households. Although an increase in prices was swiftly denounced by consumers' associations, INSEE initially adopted a conciliatory, wait-and-see position, taking the view that perceptions of an increase in inflation would be without any real foundation. It subsequently further developed the hypothesis of a gap between households' perception of the evolution of prices and the evolution of prices as reflected in the official index.

The indices of perception were not, strictly speaking, anything new. For example, a 'psychological cost of living indicator' had been in use from 1945 until the early 1960s. It was produced several times a year and constructed on the basis of the following question: "In your view, how much money does a family of four in your locality need each month in order to live?"; it was disseminated by IFOP (Chélini 1998, p. 138). It was replaced by a monthly household economic outlook survey (Camme) conducted by INSEE. It provided analysts and political decision-makers with information on households' opinions on macroeconomic trends (growth, price increases, etc.) and contributed to an index of consumer 'morale'.

Since 1996, individuals had been surveyed about their opinion of inflation over the previous six months. The following questions were put to them: 'Do you find that over the last six months prices have risen sharply/have risen moderately/have risen a little/have stagnated/have fallen?'. An overhauled version of this household economic outlook survey was introduced in 2004. The question are harmonised at the European level and canvass opinion on the general economic situation in France, over the previous 12 months and the 12 months to come (general economic situation, unemployment and inflation). Thus the survey provided information on the possible evolution of household opinion (*Informations rapides*, 28 February 2007, p. 2). A balance of opinion was calculated each year by taking the "difference between the percentages of positive and negative responses" (p. 1) and tracked over time (see Box 3.2). This time the aim of the questionnaire put to a sample of 2000 people was to provide a *quantitative* evaluation of past inflation. The initial analyses conducted by INSEE and the Banque de France assessed personal opinions on inflation, which were "both highly dispersed and on average very much higher than inflation as measured by the CPI: respondents frequently stated that the inflation rate was of the order of 15, 20 or even 25% per year" (Accardo et al. 2012).

At the same time, a report commissioned by the ECB was compiled by a number of economists under the direction of Heinz Christian Dieden (Dieden et al. 2006). Entitled *Consumer's quantitative inflation perceptions and expectations in the Euro area: a first evaluation*, it observed very clear differences in all European countries between perceptions and the official indices (cf. Fig. 3.1). The gap in France was particularly wide; between 2004 and 2010, it was permanently of the order of six percentage points (Accardo et al. 2011, p. 4).

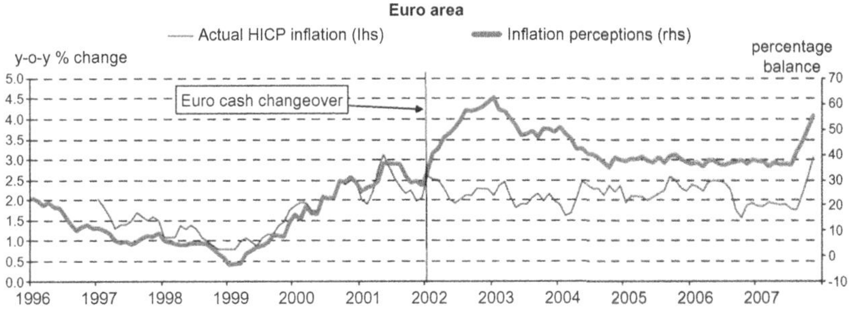

Fig. 3.1 Comparative evolution of the HICP in the Eurozone and the index of European households' perceptions of the evolution of inflation: 1998–2008. (Source: Eurostat, *in* Mariton 2008, p. 16)

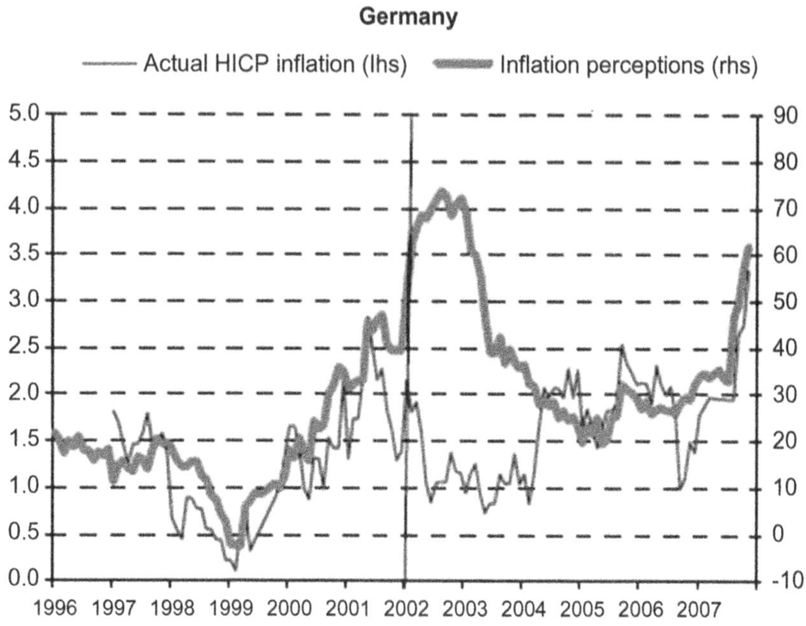

Fig. 3.2 Comparative evolution of the HICP for Germany and the index of households' perceptions of the evolution of inflation: 1998–2008. (Source: Eurostat, *in* Mariton 2008, p. 16)

However, households' assessments of the past evolution of prices improved fairly rapidly in some European countries. According to Accardo et al., inflation as perceived by households gradually declined, reaching a level consistent with inflation as measured by the CPI as early as mid-2004 in Germany (Fig. 3.2) and from 2005 onwards in Italy.

In Spain and Greece, the gaps narrowed but household perceptions of inflation remained higher than the official index. In Portugal and Ireland, after a peak in the spring of 2003, household perceptions of inflation fell back at the same time as the inflationary tensions weakened (Accardo et al. 2007, p. 71). In France, a certain degree of exceptionalism seemed to persist, since the gap between the CPI and perceptions of inflation remained wider than in the other European countries for a whole decade. It was not until 2016 that the gap seemed to narrow (Fig. 3.3).

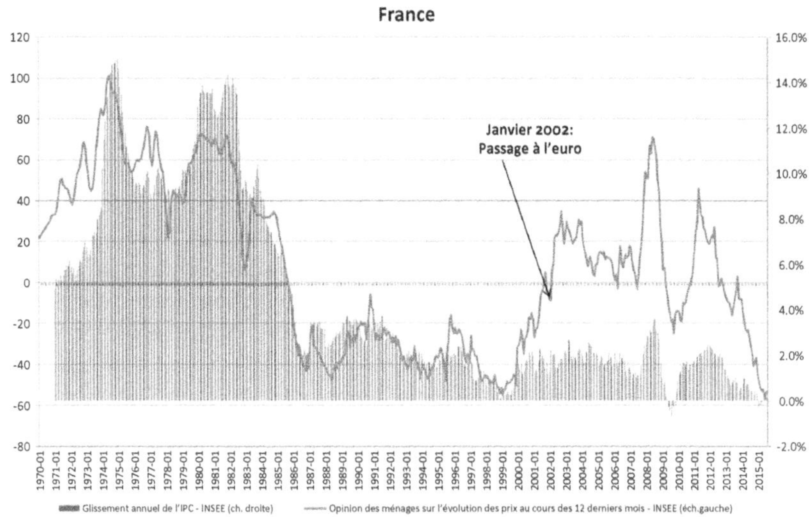

Fig. 3.3 Evolution of the gap between perceptions and the official measure of inflation. France: 1970–2016. (Source: Pionnier 2015)

2.3 *New Actors*

2.3.1 *The Large Retailers Get Involved*

During this very sensitive period, the controversy acquired a new ambassador in the shape of Michel-Edouard Leclerc, famous French director of the eponymous network of hypermarkets. Leclerc proclaimed himself the defender of households' purchasing power (thereby promoting his low-price policy), replacing the trade unions which were in retreat to some extent and whose position vis-à-vis official statistics had been tricky since the mid-1980s. Collectively, they tended usually to express fierce loyalty to their institution (Pénissat 2009, p. 42). The trade unions also argued, quite rightly, that democratic societies desperately needed solid and reliable official statistics provided by a credible body.

In February 2004, the retailer ran an explicit advertising campaign in which he challenged INSEE's 2003 diagnosis of household purchasing power. The Minister for the Economy and Finance at the time, Nicolas Sarkozy, played a crucial role in attracting public attention to this polemic, since he regularly denounced "the price rises in large-scale retailing" (Data 2009, p. 26), while at the same time directing part of his argument at the

Box 3.2 Measuring Household Perceptions of Inflation
Since 1996, INSEE has been assessing household perceptions of inflation on the basis of the following question: 'Do you find that over the last six months prices have (M1) risen sharply/have (M2) risen moderately/have (M3) risen a little/have (M4) stagnated/have (M5) fallen?'. Since 2004, this question has been asked with regard to inflation over the previous 12 months, while from 1996 to 2003 respondents were asked about inflation over the previous six months. In a second wave of questions, households are asked about their expectations of inflation with the following question: 'With reference to developments over the past 12 months, how do you think the consumer price index will change in the coming 12 months?'. The possible answers are: it will rise more rapidly/it will rise at the same rate/it will rise more slowly/it will stagnate/it will fall/I don't know.

In order to construct a synthetic indicator, INSEE then calculates balances of opinion on the basis of the difference between the share of respondents who gave a positive opinion and the share of those who gave a negative opinion, as it does for other perception-based economic outlook surveys (notably with regard to unemployment). In the present case, given the number of modalities, the median modality is allocated a weighting coefficient of 0, while the extreme modalities at either end of the range are given a coefficient of 1 and the more qualified modalities a coefficient of ½. The balance = M1 + [1/2 × M2] - [1/2 × M4] - M5. In Fig. 3.3, the scale of the balance of opinions is identified on the left-hand axis. The fact that the inflation curve and the curve of this balance of opinion are superimposed throughout the period 1974–1999 is purely conventional here and makes it possible to show the gap that has existed since the year 2000.

Supplementary questions about the evolution of the prices of a number of everyday products were added to the surveys in 2007 and 2009. A sample of households was questioned about the changes in the prices of ten products: bread, meat, beef, cooking oil, electricity bill, car repairs, petrol, telephone bill, washing machine and television. The question asked was: "Do you find that the price of this good is rising more quickly, less quickly or at the same pace as the general evolution of prices?"

(*continued*)

Box 3.2 (continued)

This measurement exercise has been supplemented since 2004 by the Camme survey, in which people's opinion of inflation is measured, this time quantitatively. A sample of 2000 household interviewed on the telephone is asked what their estimate of inflation for the year is. In 2008, for example, 3% of households put the inflation rate at 25%, while in 2010 4.5% of households were still putting it at 20%. The average gap between inflation as measured by INSEE and this personal opinion of inflation was permanently about 6 percentage points over the period 2004–2010 (Accardo et al. 2012). This survey is carried out at the European level and continued to show a clear gap between measured inflation and opinions on inflation until 2016 (Fig. 3.4).

Sources: Accardo et al. (2012), Arioli et al. (2017).

Fig. 3.4 Perception of inflation, expectations of inflation and the harmonised index of consumer prices in the European Union, 2004–2016. (Source: Arioli et al. 2017, p. 17)

allegedly excessive cost of labour. Leclerc insisted that a price index should be able to reflect the evolution of the prices of goods distributed through this type of sales outlet. Jean-Michel Charpin, the then Director-General of INSEE, responded professionally to the orders issued by the minister, Nicolas Sarkozy, who was demanding that an index for large-scale retailing be constructed in all haste. The aim of this project was to damp down the controversy with the large-scale retail sector, which had a "majority share of the market for food and other everyday consumption goods" and therefore played a decisive role "in the daily lives of French consumers" (Accardo et al. 2007, p. 71) and hence in their perception of the evolution of prices. INSEE complied in 2004, having statistically verified the feasibility of such an index and considered the appropriateness of adding it to the statistical landscape. It used available data and a restricted range of everyday consumer products (food products, home care products, personal hygiene and beauty products, etc.) (Accardo et al. 2007); INSEE accepted—on the basis that just the once wouldn't hurt—that the data were not entirely reliable since no specific survey had been carried out, so that the whole project was something of a makeshift job. The statistics thus obtained suggested large-scale retail price index had begun to rise prior to the changeover to the euro (1998/1999).

2.3.2 *The Effects of the 2007 Presidential Campaign*

The year 2007 and those immediately following it were difficult. During the 2007 presidential campaign, Nicolas Sarkozy issued the following edict: "I don't want anyone to make fun of the French any more for having price indices that are absolutely meaningless" (Data, op. cit.). This head-on attack on the credibility of INSEE's outputs forced the official statistical service to embark on more aggressive media campaigns than was its wont. Not only does this event show that the history of the price index remains inextricably linked to that of the ties between INSEE and political power but Jean-Philippe Cotis, the new Director-General of INSEE, also instituted a series of press conferences intended to provide instruction on the statistical bases of the main macroeconomic aggregates.

3 What Is the 'Right' Level of Price Inflation?

The debates on the right level of price inflation that have gone on in all European countries since the advent of the euro have brought into play a host of explanatory factors. Various arguments have been advanced, notably that there are certain products that are purchased so frequently that households' sensitivity to price rises could be greater.

3.1 *Individuals' Frequency of Purchasing*

This hypothesis can be tested by Brachinger's index. It is constructed like a CPI, apart from two major differences. Firstly, goods are weighted not by their relative shares in household budgets but by the frequency with which they are purchased. This is calculated on the basis of the family budget survey. The second difference is that those goods "whose prices increase are assigned an overweighting by a factor *K*", *K* being considered, following Tversky and Kahneman (1991), as a loss aversion coefficient. Loss aversion is a notion derived from behavioural economics that suggests that, under certain circumstances, individuals attribute greater importance to a loss than to a gain of the same value. In the tests carried out by INSEE and the Bank of France, "two values of this coefficient were tested: $K = 1,1$ and $K = 2$" (Accardo et al. 2012). They give rise to the following graph (Fig. 3.5), which shows that, *on average*, the index adjusted for frequency of purchase and which uses a strong loss aversion eliminates the gap between the price index and individuals' perceptions of it. In other words, these psychological variables serve to explain this hiatus between perceptions and the CPI.

3.2 *The Growing Inequalities Between Socio-occupational Categories*

INSEE has a long tradition of producing structural explanations for socio-economic phenomena. This is due to the technical training of its officials who are—or at least were until the 1980s—well versed in analyses that naturally combine economics and sociology. It is not surprising, therefore, that certain statisticians were fairly quick to advance the hypothesis that the growing diversity of European populations might explain the loss of confidence in the price index which, as an average, becomes a more problematic reference point when inequalities are increasing. In a lengthy report on "*La mesure du pouvoir d'achat et de sa perception par les ménages/* Measuring purchasing power and its perception by households" (Accardo et al. 2007), INSEE proposed that separate price indices should be constructed for the various socio-occupational categories, which would be compiled by adjusting the weightings in accordance with the consumption

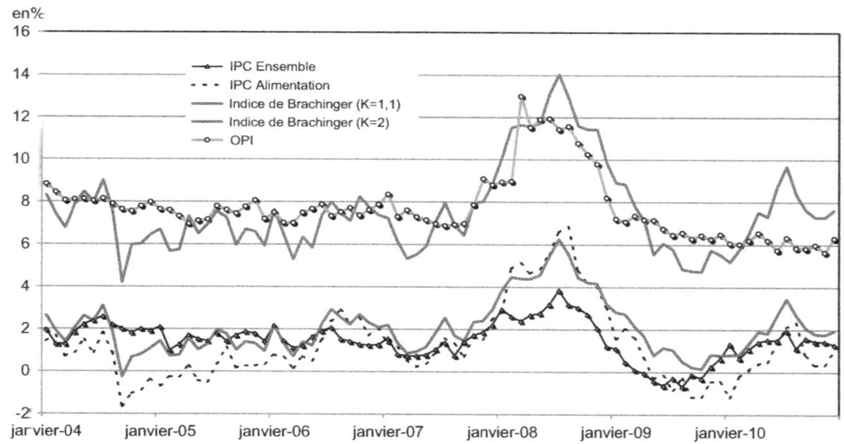

Fig. 3.5 Inflation over 12 months as measured by the CPI, the index of perceived inflation (IPI) and Brachinger's index. (Source: Accardo et al. 2012, p. 3. Sources: INSEE: Consumer price index; Camme survey; family budget survey 2006. Example: in January 2004, the rate of inflation over the previous 12 months was 2% according to the CPI. On the same date, perceived inflation (IPI) was 8.95. The Brachinger's index on the same date was 2.7% or 8.5% depending on the value adopted for the overweighting of the rising prices (parameter *K*))

structures of the different categories, which could be derived from the family budget surveys. The underlying hypothesis was that "the various socio-occupational categories are unequally exposed to price variations". Nevertheless, Accordo's results (Accardo et al. 2007 p. 75) show, somewhat surprisingly, that socio-occupational category has only a very weak influence on variations in the price index and a slightly stronger but still limited influence on the index by income per consumption unit (a consumption unit is a coefficient attributed to each household member in order to take account of economies of scale in household consumption).

One of the reasons for this relative lack of influence is that these 'categorical price indices' are calculated in a fairly rudimentary way. After all, the data used are still those pertaining to all households, with only the weightings being changed. However, modification of the budget coefficients depending on social category is not the only factor in unequal exposure to inflation. A second, undoubtedly decisive factor is the product range effect. The aim here is to take account of the fact that a blue-collar or low-skilled white-collar household does not purchase the same goods or services within the same class of products as a senior executive: not the same 'coffees', not the same 'cars', not the same 'fruit and vegetables' and not the same 'services'. These product range effects can impact on the results although the direction of their influence cannot be predicted, since the CPI surveys do not investigate the question in any further detail from this point of view, which is regrettable.

This avenue of investigation has been closed off since 2007 due to both the lack of statistical significance in the results for the differences between categorical indices and, undoubtedly, a decline in interest among experts in the question of "social classes" (Pierru and Spire 2008; Bidet et al. 2012); additional resources would be required if it were to be reopened for more detailed analysis. Incidentally, the household CPI used to index the national minimum wage was replaced some time afterwards, in 2013, by "the index of households in the first quintile of the distribution of standards of living"—further evidence in support of the argument that the question of social class has been largely excluded from statistical descriptions.

Another hypothesis—namely the extent of households' 'involuntary' expenditure—emerged and achieved a sufficiently high profile for politicians to latch on to it.

3.3 *Involuntary Expenditure: Between Old Realities and a New Concept?*

In a mandate letter addressed to Alain Quinet, the Inspector General of Finances, Christine Lagarde, the then Minister of the Economy and Finance, expressed the hope "that the Commission will address the issue of 'involuntary expenditure' by suggesting a sufficiently precise and consensual definition of this concept that can be used to calculate at regular intervals indices of the changes in the level of such expenditure over time".

The notion of an involuntary component of household expenditure, to which the unions had been drawing attention for decades, is part of the purchasing 'power' problematic (to what extent do consumers really have the power to purchase rather than an obligation to do so?) and may refer to any of a number of different situations. It may, for example, concern household consumption expenditure to which advance commitments have already been made (through a contract, a subscription or, more generally, a contractual right of access); it may also concern necessary or even vital expenditure (food, health products and services, work-related expenditure, car, etc.). The BIPE, a consultancy company that developed an indicator of involuntary expenditure, "includes in its definition costs linked to housing, compulsory insurance, public transport and loan repayments (which in accounting terms are savings), totalling 33% of gross disposable income in 2006". It is not until "these necessary or vital and involuntary components have been deducted that the 'accessible' or 'liberated' income can be determined—what some call the 'liberated purchasing power'" (BIPE 2006)—and which represents "what remains for households once they have made these involuntary payments" (Quinet 2008, p. 13).

The Quinet Commission drew up an empirical list of "fixed expenses" that included expenditure related to housing (rent, water charges and bills for gas, electricity and other domestic fuels), canteen expenses, television services (licence fee, subscriptions to pay channels), insurance (excluding life insurance) and financial services (FISIM and other financial services). On this basis, INSEE calculates that fixed expenses, the share of which is increasing spectacularly in France, rose from 14.7% in 1959 to 33.7% in 2016 (see Fig. 3.6). These involuntary or pre-committed expenditure weigh even more heavily for poor families. According to the public Department of Research, Studies, Evaluation and Statistics of the French Ministry of Health, in 2011, they represented 61% of the disposable

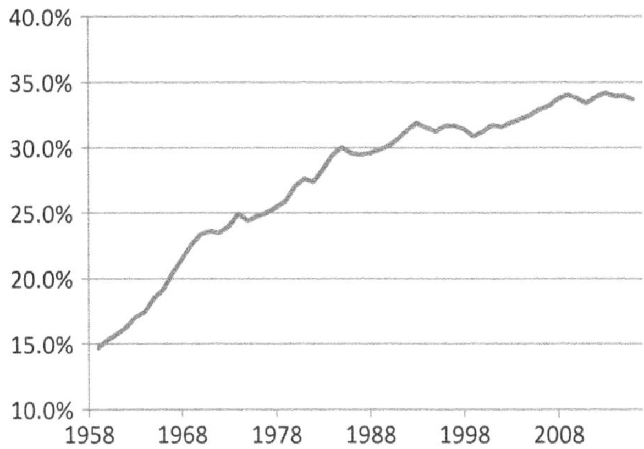

Fig. 3.6 Evolution of pre-committed expenditures in France: 1959–2016. (Source: Insee, Les comptes de la nation 2016)

income of the poor (i.e. below the poverty line), against 24% for the 25% the wealthiest.

This notion of "involuntary expenditure" can be extended to a whole series of situations in which individuals, beings located in a particular socio-institutional space, respond with purchases. This may be linked to regulatory arrangements, as already noted, particularly those put in place to internalise environmental or social costs, as well as to purchases made under social pressures (mimesis) or as a result of producer strategies. The notion of involuntary and liberated expenditure was debated internally within INSEE. In particular, it was unsettling for some of the economists attached to the prevailing notion that transactions were carried out freely and without constraint by enlightened consumers and that the price paid reflected the reality revealed by the two parties' utility.

This idea of involuntary expenditure, the extent of which is estimated in the reports cited on the basis of different definitions, is the mirror image of another problematic, that of constrained quality. If prices are truly to reflect the evolution of quality, then the market has to be free and quality has to be chosen by consumers. However, for a whole series of reasons, the launch of new goods may generate 'goodwill' for the producer, which has nothing to do with the quality of the good concerned but is due to the simple fact that consumers have no point of reference for comparison (Moati and Rochefort 2008) and that producers are seeking to re-establish forms of monopoly within their sphere of operations. Similarly, part of the quality is highly constrained by standards, rules and conventions, which may vary from one period to another (see Chap. 4).

4 An Unheard-of Response from INSEE: The Launch of an Online Individual Simulator

While the arguments around the unequal exposure to the effects of inflation, involuntary expenditure and constrained quality were explored, they gave way, nevertheless, to a hitherto unheard-of response from several European statistical bureaux.

A 'personal inflation calculator' was put on line in several countries. The idea was to enable all consumers to access a self-service simulator that they could use to calculate, more or less instantaneously, their own personal inflation rate. This device was developed in response to an assumed computational "hyper-rationality" on the part of individual consumers but was also an attempt to curb this crisis of confidence in the price index. As early as 2006, the German statistical institute (Destatis) uploaded an initial version of a personal calculator to its official site, which users could modify depending on their personal consumption structure. The initiative was reported in the journal *Sigma—The Bulletin of European Statistics* (Neutze 2006). Other national statistical offices in Europe, which at this time were holding frequent bilateral or multilateral meetings in order to quell this crisis, followed close on the German institute's heels, which gives an idea of the speed with which innovative statistical methods and the accompanying expertise circulate within Europe and internationally. In the UK as early as 2007, two statisticians at the Office for National Statistics described the introduction by the British national statistical institute of a site dedicated to the calculation of personal inflation rates on which consumers could enter their own personal consumption weightings in order to simulate their personal inflation. In France during the first quarter of 2017, INSEE drew directly on the German experience to set up bilateral meetings with the aim of stemming the loss of confidence in the price index. It launched an online simulator that could be accessed by anyone surfing the Internet (see Box 3.3 below).

In developing these personal simulators and adopting this type of graphical representation, the statistical institutes had several objectives in mind. They were trying to keep hyper-rational consumers happy, to calm down the public controversies and to help restore the index's legitimacy,

Box 3.3 The Soothing Effect of the Curves

The way of presenting trends can be debated; if the current year is adopted as base 100, then the graph depicted in Fig. 3.7 gives the impression that prices are converging. On the contrary, in the example of the graph, the official annual inflation rate was 1.4%, while for the fictitious consumer (who has no car and consumes few semi-durable or leisure goods) it was 1.9% per year from 2000 onwards. In total, nevertheless, the gap between the official inflation rate and the personal inflation rate was 10 percentage points over a period of 16½ years (inflation of 26% according to the official index and 36% according to the fictitious individual's personal inflation rate). If the year 2000 had been adopted as base 100, the gap would have been widening rather than narrowing.

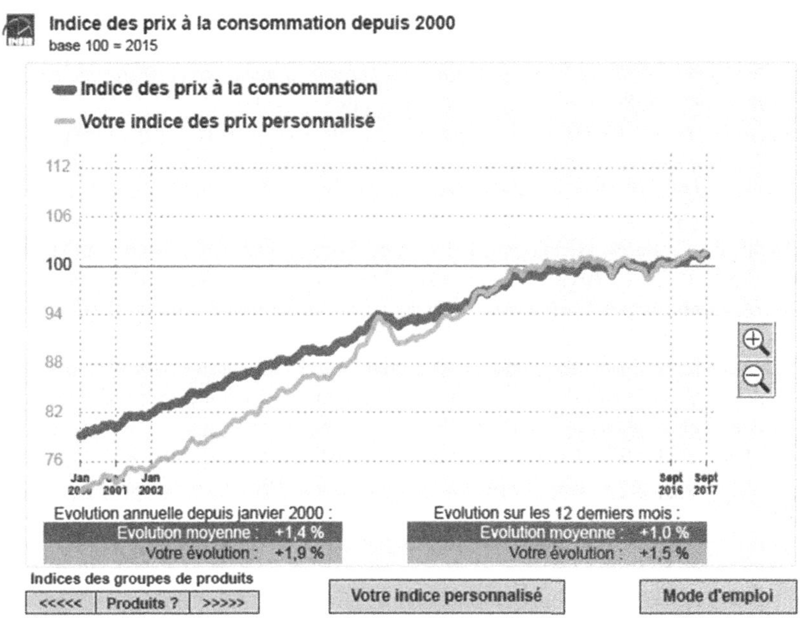

Fig. 3.7 INSEE's simulator, fictitious example. (Source: Personal test on a personalised CPI and the official CPI. *Downloaded October 9, 2017*)

as well as to give legitimacy to the idea that a personal cost of living index would be more appropriate. By making the index more relevant to individuals, these official statistical institutes also thought they could safeguard the legitimacy of the process by which the average index was produced. This new statistical tool also reflected the prevailing mode of state governance, in which the number of data processing centres was increasing and evaluative systems were becoming increasingly individualised (Desrosières 2008). A price index calculated by each individual becomes a personalised mode of statistical description which, without having any legal status, enables each person to get their lives in order by behaving rationally and optimally. These devices promulgate an impoverished conception of official statistics and it might well be wondered whether they do not also divest official statistical institutes of the broader outlook required for the production of the collective cognitive mechanisms economic agents need for the purpose of coordination (Jany-Catrice 2018).

References

Accardo, J., P. Chevalier, G. Forgeot, A. Friez, D. Guédès, F. Lenglart, and V. Passeron. 2007. *La perception du pouvoir d'achat et sa réception par les ménages*, 58–86. Insee: l'économie française.

Accardo, J., C. Célérier, N. Herpin, and D. Irac. 2011. L'inflation perçue. *Économie et Statistique* 447: 4–31.

———. 2012. L'inflation telle qu'elle est perçue par les ménages. *Insee Analyses*, no. 5, juillet.

Arioli, R., C. Bates, H. Dieden, I. Duca, R. Friz, C. Gayer, G. Kenny, A. Meyler, and I. Pavlova. 2017. *EU Consumers' Quantitative Inflation Perceptions and Expectations: An Evaluation*. European Central Bank, Occasional Paper Series, no. 186, April.

Barret, Ch., J. Bonotaux, and F. Magnien. 2003. La mesure des prix dans les domaines de la santé et de l'action sociale : quelques problèmes méthodologiques. *Économie et Statistique* 361: 3–25.

Bidet, A., et al. 2012. Ce que la socio-économie fait aux classes sociales: renouveau ou disparition? *Revue française de socio-économie* 10 (2): 219–223.

BIPE. 2006. Le pouvoir d'achat effectif du consommateur - estimation 2006 et prévision 20073 dossier de presse, septembre.

Chélini, M.-P. 1998. *Inflation, État et opinion en France de 1944 à 1952, Comité pour l'histoire économique et financière de la France*. Coll. "Études générales".

Data. 2009. *Le grand trucage. Comment le gouvernement manipule les statistiques*. La Découverte.

Desrosières, A. 2008. *L'argument statistique. Tome I : Pour une sociologie historique de la quantification. Tome II: Gouverner par les nombres.* Paris: Éditions des Mines ParisTech, coll. "Sciences sociales".
Dieden, H., R. Friz, V. Genre, G. Le Breton, and S. Linden. 2006. *Consumer's Quantitative Inflation Perceptions and Expectations in the Euro Area: A First Evaluation.* Report to the European Central Bank, European Commission.
ILO, IMF, OECD, the European Communities, United Nations, Eurostat, The World Bank. 2004. *Consumer Price Index Manual. Theory and Practice.* Geneva: ILO.
Jany-Catrice, F. 2018. Conflicts in the Calculation and Use of the Price Index—The Case of France. *Cambridge Journal of Economics* 42 (4): 963–986.
Lemoine, B. 2013. *Résister aux mesures européennes. Les États à l'épreuve de la surveillance statistique des finances publiques.* Quaderni, février.
Mariton, H. 2008. *Rapport d'information de la mission d'information commune sur la mesure des grandes données économiques et sociales.* Rapport de l'Assemblée nationale, no. 815.
Moati, Ph., and R. Rochefort. 2008. *Mesurer le pouvoir d'achat, Rapport pour le CAE.* Paris: La Documentation française.
Neutze, M. 2006. *Calculate Your Own Inflation Rate.* Sigma. The Bulletin of European Statistics, no. 1.
Pénissat, E. 2009. *L'État des chiffres. Sociologie du service de statistique et des statisticiens du ministère du Travail et de l'Emploi (1945–2008).* Thèse de sociologie à l'EHESS.
Pierru, E., and A. Spire. 2008. Le crépuscule des catégories socioprofessionnelles. *Revue française de science politique* 58: 457–481.
Pionnier, P.-A. 2015. Coût de la vie: perception et réalité statistique. *Communication aux Journées d'économie de Lyon*, 13 octobre.
Quinet, A. 2008. Rapport de la commission "Mesure du pouvoir d'achat des ménages" remis à Mme Christine Lagarde, ministre de l'Économie, des Finances et de l'Emploi, 6 février.
Savage, J. 2005. *Making the EMU, the Politics of Budgetary Surveillance and the Enforcement of Maastricht.* Oxford: Oxford University Press.
Tinel, B. 2016. *Dette publique: sortir du catastrophisme.* Paris: Raisons d'agir.
Tversky, A., and D. Kahneman. 1991. Loss Aversion in Riskless Choice: A Reference-Dependent Model. *The Quarterly Journal of Economics* 106 (4): 1039–1061.

CHAPTER 4

The Quality Effect

The statistical treatment of quality certainly merits a full chapter of its own. Questions around contemporary methods of constructing the price index are not, of course, limited to the quality issue. As already noted, the question of product renewal, for example, is an equally thorny one. However, the treatment of quality has been an object of bitter debates and regular innovations for more than 50 years. Since the evolution of the price of a basket of fixed goods of constant quality was originally at the heart of the measure, any variation in quality has to be treated in such a way that it does not appear as a change in the (pure) price of the good. In an ideal world, therefore, if the price of a computer goes up by 10% between two periods but at the same time its quality is considered to have increased by 8%, then the increase in its pure price should be only 2% and the CPI should record only this 2% increase and not the nominal increase of 10%; the same applies to yoghurt (if it becomes organic), cars (if their functionality is improved or their life span declines) and, ultimately, to all the goods and services included in the index whose quality varies over time. The difficulty lies in the very idea that a precise figure can be put on the increase in quality, whether it be '8%' or any other value.

The early debates on including quality in measurements of price changes date from the Second World War and took place in the USA. During this period, the American trade unions were in dispute with the official statistics bureau over its failure to take account of the *decline* in product quality in the price index (Stapleford 2009, p. 309). In their view, this decline in

F. Jany-Catrice, *A Political Economy of the Measurement of Inflation*,
https://doi.org/10.1007/978-3-030-59940-9_4

quality should have been reflected in a concomitant increase in the measure of inflation. After all, even if prices seemed to be stable, if product quality declines then consumers in fact experience an implicit price increase. These ideas were originally taken up by the American left with a view to taking better account of inequalities in exposure to inflation and increasing the purchasing power of the poorest members of society (op. cit., p. 384).

The treatment of the quality effect in official price statistics reflects both a process of trial and error and economic history, or more specifically the history of economic thought and of the discipline itself. Economics became significantly more professionalised after the Second World War and gradually grew into the preserve of experts. From the end of the 1950s onwards, part of the economics profession in the USA gradually equipped the price index with a framework derived from microeconomic consumer theory. We will examine this framework, taking as our starting point the Boskin Report, which left a lasting mark on the debates.

1 The Boskin Report (1996) and the Idea of "Overstated" Inflation

As the role played by economic policies expanded from the end of the 1950s onwards, official statistics were being produced with a view to creating a coherent macroeconomic framework (Stapleford 2009, p. 312). The 1959 report by Ruggles and Rees had already given an account of the influence American economists wished to exert on the establishment of a price index that would be close to a cost of living index. During the presidency of the Democrat Jimmy Carter, economists and politicians revived this idea, notably through Alfred Kahn, "President Carter's inflation fighter in his capacity as head of the Council on Wage and Price Stability" (Wahl 1982, p. 497). On behalf of the working classes, Kahn recommended, as the French Minister of the Economy and Finance Michel Bérégovoy was to do several years later in respect of access to cheap credit, that the American CPI should be revised in order to move it in the direction of a cost of living index. Most of the recommendations were taken up in 1996 by the Boskin Commission.

1.1 *The Contents of the Boskin Report*

Alan Greenspan, then chair of the Federal Reserve, testified before Congress in January 1995 on the question of the CPI. In his testimony, he argued that the American CPI overstated the annual rate of inflation by approximately one percentage point. His argument led the American Senate to commission a report in 1996 from Stanford economics professor Michael Boskin, not in order to discover whether the CPI did indeed overstate inflation but to estimate the degree of overstatement and to identify the biases responsible for it (Baker 1998, p. 81). Certain economists who, at the time, were somewhat cautious about the very idea of overstatement, particularly J. Triplett and J. Norwood of the Bureau of Labor Statistics (BLS), were not invited to join the commission, nor did the commission organise any public debates. Nevertheless, the Boskin Report attracted considerable media attention both in the USA and internationally.

The political and economic context in mid-1990s America was favourable to such reforms of the methodology used to construct the index. Apart from the fact that the period saw the end of the Cold War, the structural deficit of the American balance of payments and the increasingly strong challenges to the dollar's status as a reference currency (Théret 2010, p. 149) were all factors that encouraged policy makers to hunt for sources of deficit reductions. The first part of the report actually refers explicitly to the deterioration in the American federal deficit and to the need to reduce public expenditure, Boskin et al. adding (p. 3): "Congress and the President must decide whether they wish to continue the widespread substantial overindexing of various federal spending programs and features of the tax code".

In allying itself with these mainstream economists arguing for reform of the index, the American government acquired a veritable policy lever, all the more so since, according to the forecasts of those seeking to overturn the status quo, this supposed overstatement was likely to increase the American federal deficit by 100 billion dollars in 2008 alone.

While it was not very innovative in conceptual terms, since the NBER Report chaired by George Stigler in 1961 had already provided the main arguments for a possible overstatement of inflation, the report attracted tremendous publicity because of the results it produced. The huge media coverage the Boskin Report generated was due to its *quantification* of the gaps between the price index as actually constructed and the one that 'should' be constructed—according to economists—in order to bring it closer to a cost of living index. It was this quantification that circulated widely in the media and in people's minds: the report noted that inflation

Box 4.1 The Link Between the Measure of Inflation and Public Deficits in France

The arguments put forward by the various parties in France seeking to elucidate the link between the measurement of inflation and public deficits are of the same order as those advanced in the USA 20 years earlier: reacting to the arguments put forward by Philippe Moati and Robert Rochefort (2008), who in their report advanced the hypothesis that the official price index might be lower than it should be, Jacques Delpla asked: "Does the government really want the ECB to take into account, in drawing up its monetary policy, price indices showing a significantly higher level of inflation than the current PCI?" (Delpla, p. 165). He added (p. 166): "Indices of this kind, showing a higher level of inflation, would require a re-evaluation of the minimum social security benefits and welfare payments" (p. 166). In conclusion, he insisted: "If INSEE were to publish several price indices that showed inflation to be higher, the demands for an uprating of welfare benefits and minimum social security benefits would cause the public deficits to increase a little more".

had been overstated by about 1.1% per year in 1996 and by 1.3% per year for the previous ten years.

The major sources of bias in the CPI identified by the Commission were linked to (a) substitution practices in the purchase of goods (0.4% bias per annum) in the event of changes in relative prices, (b) outlet substitution practices (0.1% per annum), (c) the increasingly frequent introduction of new goods into consumption structures and (d) the idea of taking better account of the increased quality of these new goods (the overall bias for these two factors was put at 0.8% per annum). The quality to which Boskin referred concerned above all the quality associated with the introduction of new goods into consumption structures and not that associated with a general increase (or decline) in quality (Schultze and Mackie 2002, p. 115). The procedure adopted was to compare the CPI to the geometric mean of the micro (or macro) indices. With an arithmetic mean, after all, the hypothesis is that consumers respond quickly to changes in relative prices, the underlying idea being that there is no difference in terms of utility or well-being whether one eats beef or chicken or substitutes a premium price yoghurt for a branded one. This hypothesis was adopted on the basis, firstly, that the market is the vector for the revelation of preferences and, secondly, that the substitution between goods is perfect (Cobb-Douglas utility).

1.2 The Post-Boskin Years in France

In France, paradoxically, the debate was imported following the 1996 Boskin Commission Report by progressive economists who were interested initially in the indicators' ability to provide a different representation of wealth (Gadrey 1996). The economist Jean Gadrey tended to highlight the Boskin Commission's fairly radical proposals for dealing with the overstatement of inflation. Although he was certainly not in sympathy with Boskin's political project, Gadrey emphasised the proposed innovations for the measurement of outputs and results, which required a certain inventiveness in order to go beyond the measurements used in national accounts in activities where the very idea of unit of output is meaningless, notably in healthcare and education (see Box 4.2 below).

The concerns of INSEE statisticians centred on a possible loss of confidence in the index if the Boskin Report were to be favourably received in France (Jany-Catrice 2018). INSEE reacted officially by publishing two articles simultaneously, one by François Lequiller dans *Économie et Statistique*, the other by Michel Glaude, then INSEE's director of demographic and social statistics, in *La Revue française du marketing*. Glaude had no qualms about declaring that "the American debate seems to have got out of hand"; some of the criticisms smacked "of political opportunism" and of "Alan Greenspan's excessive adroitness in justifying a monetary policy that in fact contents itself with an annual increase in retail prices of 2 to 3%" (Glaude 1997, p. 20). For his part, François Lequiller, at the time "deputy head of INSEE's department of consumer prices, resources and living conditions and in charge of the French consumer prices index", who had just spent several years in the USA at the IMF, penned a particularly detailed piece. In this article, to which academic researchers and trade unionists continue to refer 20 years on, Lequiller takes the view that France is protected from such overstatements and that Michael Boskin should have refrained from putting a figure on the "bias": "To put any figure at all on this problem in the current state of our knowledge is hardly reasonable" (Lequiller 1997, p. 16); he even insisted that "In a case like this, the statistician's response must be to acknowledge his ignorance and to work to reduce it and not to indulge in risky estimations" (op. cit., p. 18). Lequiller acknowledges, furthermore, that most of the estimates in the Boskin Report hinge

Box 4.2 The Boskin Report and Measures of Well-Being

The Boskin Report (1996), which was presented to the US Senate's Finance Committee in 1996, focuses primarily on the various forms of bias in the measurement of inflation. This bias is even regarded as "the fourth largest federal program, after social security, healthcare and defense" (p. 2). In doing so, Boskin established that the volume of GDP and growth were understated, confirming 20 years earlier the arguments advanced by Aghion et al. (2017).

In making proposals for the measurement of the volumes of certain services and of their impacts, Boskin goes beyond this accounting debate. While he champions the idea of a cost of living index (COLI), Boskin also declares "There are still other issues that would in principle apply to obtaining a true cost of living index (COLI). Consider two examples: the negative effects of higher crime rates and the concomitant purchases of security devices and higher insurance premiums and the positive effects of improvements in information technology that permit a parent to work at home when a child is ill" (p. 26). The way of dealing with what he calls externalities, such as "colder winters", the appearance of "AIDS" (this was the beginning of the 1990s), or even the rise in the "crime rate" and the divorce rate, is not specified, but he encourages researchers to investigate these questions in greater detail in future.

As far as the results of this report are concerned, says Boskin, undoubtedly risking criticism for speaking out so boldly, the "good" elements outweigh the "bad" and society is advancing. In his view, it is in the area of the environment and healthcare that things have progressed significantly in the USA. There follows a paragraph declaring, in an almost lyrical manner, how far American society has progressed in environmental terms compared with the 1950s and 1960s (e.g. "the rapid spread of central air conditioning has made possible a substantial movement of households to the southern and south-western states"). All things considered, the visionary Boskin notes that pollution, crime, suicide and divorce "have reached a plateau" (p. 49) and "in the case of pollution and crime seem actually to have reversed direction, thus recently improving the quality of life".

on the problem of product substitution but that, with regard to a certain number of other aspects (product quality, estimation of service activities, the tension between constant utility and a fixed basket of goods, etc.), improvements can still be envisaged, but without predicting the +/- sign that might affect the index. Several years later, Eurostat was to adopt an even more explicit positions when it declared "the argument put forward in the Boskin Report, which is based on the theory of the cost of living index, does not apply, however interesting it may be, to the HICP, which is a Laspeyres-type index designed to measure inflation, and the hypotheses underlying the theory are not in general verified" (Eurostat 2001, p. 14). Nevertheless, Lequiller glimpses three ways in which the index might be improved and which were subsequently to constitute three separate reforms. The first was to accelerate the process of adopting macroeconomic methods (hedonic analysis, see Sect. 3 below) "[over and above calculations on micro computers], this avenue continues to be explored and an econometric method for estimating quality effects will soon be operational for certain durable goods (dishwashers notably)". The second was further harnessing of the synergies between European statistical institutes. The third and final improvement lay in greater use of the data generated by private market research companies, which "will probably feature among future solutions for correcting substitution biases at a detailed level as well as those attributable to new distribution channels" (Lequiller 1997, p. 24).

2 The Objectivation of Quality: Between Interpretations and Modelling

In practice, statistics is located somewhere between the necessary use of theoretical rigour and a pressing need for pragmatism in order to make visible the 'real world' that it seeks to formulate. Statistical offices are required to define the empirical rules for establishing the connections required to compare the prices of different objects of equivalent quality (Piriou 1992). Some of the methods for dealing with quality are set down in the 2004 ILO Manual (ILO et al. 2004). This manual explains how to make an adjustment or discount between the apparent evolution of prices and the evolution of the pure price stripped of changes in quality. A distinction is made in the literature between so-called implicit and explicit methods of adjustment. The use of one or other of these different methods is a matter of know-how and of technical contingencies, as well as of ideas about what constitutes a 'quality' good or service, reflecting the fact that any measurement of quality is inevitably based on conventions.

2.1 *Implicit Methods of Dealing with Quality*

In the USA, the implicit approaches have been set out at some length in the various manuals and a number of studies, for example those by Moulton and Moses (1997) have estimated the share of goods whose prices are subjected to statistical processing of one kind or another. To the best of our knowledge, this is not the case in France, which may be attributed to the index's particularly sensitive history in France and the ensuing tradition of confidentiality. The lack of legislation laying down methodological norms for the construction of the index in France stands in sharp contrast to the huge volume of norms produced at European level.

The direct method of comparison. In this method, it is assumed that there is no change in quality, even though the good or service whose variation in price over time is being observed is different. The change is regarded as sufficiently insignificant in terms of quality for the good in question to be regarded as equivalent to that observed in the previous period. This may be the case if there has been a minor change in packaging or, in the case of clothes, a change in colour or style (Schultze and Mackie 2002, p. 116). If there has been a change in price (of, e.g. 3%), this is recorded in full as a price increase. Part of the debate provoked by the Boskin Commission is linked to what, in Boskin's view, is the overly large share of goods deemed to be directly comparable (65% of goods according to Moulton, op. cit.), which would cause increases in quality to be understated. It should be noted, nevertheless, that this affirmation by Boskin is based on the assumption that all the changes not taken into account improve rather than worsen the quality of the good or service in question. In all the other implicit methods, the good or service observed over time is regarded as sufficiently different to be dealt with by one of the following methods.

The overlap method is based on the following principle: when the quality is regarded as sufficiently different, then the good in question is regarded as a new one (e.g. switchover to colour televisions or from ordinary vegetables to organic produce). When this new good is introduced into the basket to replace the previous one, the difference in the relative price between the old and the new good is observed "at the precise moment the first one disappears and the second one replaces it". In this case, as arbitrarily as in the previous case, this difference is imputed *entirely* to a difference in quality (ILO et al. 2004). The ILO et al. (2004) suggest that this method is very widely used throughout the world, whereas Moulton and Moses (1997) reckon it is used relatively little in the USA.

The radical difference in treatment between the direct comparison and overlap methods shows the extent to which the decision as to whether or not to describe a variation in quality as a new product has a considerable impact on the statistical treatment of price changes.

The overall mean imputation method is used when the substitute good or service differs to an even greater extent from its predecessor. In this case, the break between the two series is, as it were, "plugged" by assuming that, at the moment of the changeover, the change in price is comparable to the general evolution of prices: "The pure price difference between the good that disappears and the one that is going to replace it is equal to the average variations in price for the goods that remain on sale" (ILO et al. 2004).

The class mean imputation method is the one most frequently used by statisticians, particularly at INSEE. It is based on the same principle as the previous method. This time, however, the imputed rate is that of the class (or of an equivalent class) of the good that is being replaced. Generally, a waiting period is observed before the new good is introduced into the base, in order to ensure, firstly, that a sufficient volume has been consumed and, secondly, that its price in the product life cycle has fallen. The method adopted is often similar to the establishment of a price on a fictitious basis, that is on the basis of its equivalent already on the market. "Use of this method", said J.-P. Piriou mischievously, "meant that the television was introduced with the aid of the index for radio sets and the dishwasher with the aid of that for large household durables" (Piriou 1992, p. 57).

According to Boskin, this method tends to understate the increase in quality at the time of the changeover because the fictitious adjustment is carried out on the basis of goods that are far advanced in their life cycles; others (Moulton and Moses 1997, or Triplett 1997), in contrast, reach the opposite conclusion. For them, companies often take advantage of an innovation in order to restore their margins. Consequently, using the average variation in the prices of goods whose characteristics have not changed as a fictitious basis for adjustment understates the increase in the price of the good or service in question.

2.2 *The Explicit Methods*

The explicit methods are based on the idea that there are objectifiable quality criteria. If the variation in quality takes the form of a modification of physical characteristics (e.g. a product regarded as purer or a change in the product's chemical composition), the ILO et al. state that there is "considerable scope for the judicious, or common sense, application of relatively straightforward quality adjustments of this kind" (ILO et al. 2004, p. 35).

The first of these methods is based on the idea that changes in product quality add to production costs. The change in the cost of producing a standard unit as reported by the manufacturers and which improves the functionality of the good or service (e.g. the cost of introducing airbags) is subtracted from the change in price observed by consumers. In its most sophisticated variant, this method is known as the 'options cost' method and is used when the new variety of goods identified incorporates characteristics that used to be optional. This method is generally applied to products such as cars, multi-option insurance policies and packages of goods and services for tourists. A discount is applied to the observed price, namely the cost (or price) of the option. Moati and Rochefort report that, in reality, "only 50% of the price of the option is counted in order to take account of the savings generated by mass production" (2008, p. 76).

Not only does the discount of 50% seem, here too, to be determined to some extent by convention but the data on costs and quality in this type of explicit method are generally derived from experts or even producers themselves, notably via the catalogues that provide some of the product specifications. Thus this method has a certain degree of efficiency in the case of observable modifications to simple characteristics (ILO et al., p. 35) that leave no doubt as to the direction of the variation in quality. However, it leaves numerous questions unresolved, among them the fact that certain options are imposed, whether because of the producer's product positioning strategy or for regulatory reasons. The fact that they may then be classified as a quality effect should be a matter for discussion. Moreover, this way of evaluating quality gives an inaccurate estimate of the share of the change in production costs attributable to consolidation of the company's margins rather than to an increase in what could be a pure price. Producers' innovation strategies are aimed at reconstructing non-competitive spaces in markets. Finally, these methods cannot properly be applied to a high share of service activities, in which the very notion of a standard product unit poses some formidable problems (Gadrey 1996; see Box 4.3 below).

The hedonic method has since the 1940s been regarded as one of the most reputable and promising of the explicit methods. In 2004, the international organisations issued yet another plea in its favour and recommended that national statistical bureaux should use it as much as possible. The example of computers is very frequently highlighted (see below).

Box 4.3 In Search of Standard 'Product' Units

The measurement of price changes by means of price indices is meaningless unless they can be compared over time (and in space). Comparison in space requires the use of purchasing power parities (PPPs), which are not dealt with in this book, even though there are similarities from a methodological point of view and the political disputes and sensitivities around PPPs are just as fierce.

Price gathering and the technical value of such exercises have been a matter of debate for historians since time immemorial. The medievalist Julien Demade (2018), for example, has described the exercises in conversion into a standard and contemporary unit of account (per kilo, per litre, etc.) that are required—where variations in units of measurement were commonplace throughout the Middle Ages—in order to produce scientifically valid price data. However, the question of the standard unit of measurement is not limited to the ability to undertake quantity conversions. In a high share of service activities in particular, the very notion of a 'standard unit' simply does not have the meaning it has in a world in which volumes of goods, particularly standardised goods, play a major part. Let us take a few examples. What might the reference point be for the unit of consumption in banking services? Or in telecommunications or healthcare? In a very detailed article published in October 1991 issue of the excellent but now sadly defunct journal *Courrier de la statistique*, Gérald Petit outlines the main changes in the pricing of medical services in the 1980s. Medical services are divided into codified procedures. These procedures are not identified unprompted, without premeditation, as a litre of milk, a suit or a car would be, although it should be noted that even in the case of such seemingly commonplace examples, their inclusion in the CPI has been the occasion for lively debates. These procedures are social constructs, the result of legislation and bargaining between the medical profession and the French National Health Insurance Fund. Moreover, although they can be identified separately in the legislation and schedules of procedures, in professional practice they are frequently performed as grouped procedures (e.g. as is the case in cardiology or radiology). Petit describes how, for reasons of statistical impracticability, these grouped procedures were excluded from the CPI in the 1990s (p. 44).

2.3 *Services Are Affected*

To a greater or lesser extent, all the methods have to face the question of ascertaining to what degree a change to a good is sufficiently substantial for it to be regarded as a new good and to what degree this change may be attributable to a variation in quality. In the literature, this question mainly but not solely applies to goods. For example, the transfer of doctors in private practice from sectors covered by the national health scheme to sectors not so covered and their treatment in official statistics in 1990 are absolutely symptomatic of the hesitations and of the socio-political vision that is inevitably imposed on changes.

Box 4.4 Price Effect or Quality Effect? The Case of the Move from Sector 1 to Sector 2 in Private Medical Practice

"When a medical practitioner moves from one type of contractual arrangement to another (particularly from sector I to sector II) and, following that move, the prices they charge change in the course of a given month, should the quality of the services provided be deemed to have changed immediately? If the answer is yes, then the practitioner's new charges have to be taken into account in categories other than those in which they were originally included, namely those relating to the practitioner's new contractual sector. There will not be a price increase if the new charges are close to the average of the fees charged by their colleagues in the new sector for the same services. Otherwise, there will not be any reason to regard that doctor's services as being different from those provided by other doctors in their original contractual sector. The new charges will be assigned to the same categories as previously. On the other hand, there will be a price increase if those charges are higher than the average of the fees charged by their colleagues in their original sector. It is unlikely that a doctor will change their working practices on the very same day that they change their contractual arrangements and it seems reasonable to assume that they will adapt over time to the practices of colleagues who have been practising according to the new contractual arrangements for longer. Naturally, it is very difficult, impossible even, to quantify this change in working practices in order to make it a calculable item of information. (…) INSEE has chosen the second option, taking the view that, statistically, the move from one contractual arrangement to another is not reflected immediately in changes in the quality of the medical services provided" (Petit 1991, p. 45).

2.4 *The Uncertain and Convention-Based Nature of Quality*

The statistical treatment of quality is constrained by its uncertain and convention-based nature and by the individual and collective subjectivities brought to bear in interpreting it.

Whereas it is considered in the classification hypothesis that "the 'essential' qualities of goods are defined unambiguously, exogenously, as embedded in the goods themselves" (Eymard-Duvernay 1989, p. 332), quality is de facto the inextricable result of producers' perceptions and of consumers' subjective perceptions as well as of norms, collective standards, legislation and hidden conventions that inevitably vary over time. This is what the economist from the French *convention* school, François Eymard-Duvernay, investigated so remarkably. The definition of and ways of measuring quality result from various forms of agreement. The mechanism through which they obtain social validation may be industrial (as determined by the producers), market-based (extolling of individual subjectivity), civic or domestic (in which case the validation is a product of interpersonal relations). In fact, the measurement of quality embodies all these states to some extent; however, it is certainly in the statistical treatment of quality that disputes around the representation of wealth come to confront each other. This becomes evident when the question of quality arises: what is the quality that matters? Are lists of the technical specifications of goods to be constructed? Should the relational characteristics of services be taken into account? Or the impacts of consumption on well-being (and if so, what form of well-being?)? Should the durability of goods be taken into account?

Although statisticians would have loved production standards to be "objectivised" and "taken out of the reach of the various actors" (Eymard-Duvernay 1989, p. 346), in fact they have long been embodied in the protocols used by interviewers as well as by INSEE statisticians in their data processing. What are we to make of the substitute purchases made at different outlets, and in particular the transition from traditional outlets to hypermarkets or hard discounters? One option is to consider that they are *not the same products*, since the quality varies; this is the point of view espoused, for example, by Lequiller in 1997. In this case, the reduction in prices can be imputed in full to a reduction in quality and the price in the index remains constant. Alternatively, the quality in both types of outlet can be regarded as comparable, which is the view taken by certain experts and studies of the quality of the goods sold (OQALI) (an organisation established in 2008 by the ministries of Agriculture, Health and Consumer Affairs, with implementation by INRA and ANSES, 2015 study). In that case, the reduction in price will be regarded as a genuine reduction in price. In practice, because of this wide range of choices and the presuppositions that accompany them, producers of official statistics are obliged to put the methodologies into some sort of hierarchical order, which forces them to make rulings, without being able completely—far from it—to dispense with interpretative judgements.

3 The Hedonic Method: Between Promises and Disappointments

Hedonic analysis has often been regarded as the ideal method for settling statistical disputes around quality.

It was first used in agriculture (Waugh 1929) and then in manufacturing industry with the seminal 1938 studies by Andrew Court (Goodman 1998). This economist was recruited by the automobile manufacturers. His work consisted of using econometric techniques to demonstrate that, if the increase in the quality of certain of the automobiles' characteristics was taken into account, then the price paid by consumers was lower than the nominal price paid on purchase. By arguing that, contrary to appearances, sale prices had been contained, he was hoping to persuade the public authorities in the 1930s to act to the advantage of the automobile industry by reducing the "constraints and charges" that weighed heavily on it (Stapleford 2009, p. 315). The method remained confidential until the 1960s. It was then popularised in the USA, notably by Zvi Griliches of the NBER. The hedonic techniques he promoted met with considerable success in the USA because the method links market prices to a product's characteristics (i.e. to the various dimensions of quality), which suggests that if the judgement of statisticians is called on, it is only to a limited extent. This period also coincided with the rise to prominence and legitimacy of econometrics as an analytical tool in economics, particularly in the analysis of consumer behaviour. The main obstacles to the use of the hedonic method are attributed to the limitations of data collection and the inability of statistics to capture all the characteristics of goods.

3.1 *The Principle of the Hedonic Method*

The hedonic method met with considerable success in the USA in the 1960s and 1970s and was legitimised by Lancaster's characteristics demand theory, which posits that complex goods can be decomposed into a variety of characteristics that can then undergo objectivised measurement. Its starting hypothesis is that goods offered for sale in a market are purchased primarily for the characteristics that define those goods (in the case of a washing machine, e.g. its power, energy consumption, colour and so on) and that the price is a function of a good's vector of characteristics (in other words, the price of a good j can be written $p_j = f(c_1^j; c_2^j \ldots; c_i^j \ldots; c_k^j)$). The method involves estimating each variation in the price of the various characteristics associated with this good, characteristics that are judged to be useful or pleasing (hence the term hedonic) to consumers. Once the data on a good's characteristics and prices have been collected, an implicit price is allotted to each of the characteristics. In the case of a laptop computer, for example, the following might apply: price = α [size of hard drive] + β [RAM] + γ [screen size] + δ[weight] + ε[battery life], etc. Thus the method combines the judgement of the market, the statements of the producers who set out the specifications and the judgements of the statisticians who select the variables to be introduced and the meaning to attribute to them in terms of quality. In econometric terms, the hedonic method consists of multiple regressions. The regression coefficients value the characteristics and are regarded as the implicit prices of those characteristics. In theory at least, this makes it possible to estimate the implicit price of an air conditioning unit, of the added power output of an iron or the multiple characteristics of a dwelling (both its own specific characteristics such as size, number of rooms, age and so on and its environmental characteristics, such as the presence of a nearby park or its location a neighbourhood with a high or low crime rate). The implicit prices are allocated to the actual characteristics of the new good in order to estimate what its price should have been if the price had simply been a direct reflection of its specific characteristics. "The difference between the theoretical and actual price makes it possible to separate the quality effect from the 'pure' price variation" (Moati and Rochefort 2008, p. 76). This method seems suited to taking account of the variations in certain characteristics, but it requires very regular re-estimations of the regression coefficients and is unable to deal with cases in which new characteristics emerge (Ibid.).

In an ideal hedonic function, all the qualitative and quantitative variables that affect a consumer's utility have to be taken into account, quality being defined as the variation in the consumer's utility. In practice, however, objectifying the quality criteria is an altogether trickier proposition. This is because, firstly, the procedure is an econometric one and is therefore still convention-based, since the statisticians concerned are drawing on 'technical and practical conventions'. As already noted, the information on the characteristics of these products is often, or even in most cases, provided by the producers: in the "options cost" method, the statisticians consult the car makers' catalogues that list the characteristics and the price of each one (Lequiller 1997). What are the consequences of this? Some studies show that manufacturers tend, in these signalling effects, to overestimate the production costs required to increase quality (Kokoski 1993, p. 35). A panel of the American committee on national statistics, chaired by Charles Schultze, who edited a major report at the beginning of the 2000s (Schultze and Mackie 2002), recommended that the BLS and the Bureau of Economic Analysis (BEA) should be (more) cautious in using the hedonic method (p. 6) and that hedonic techniques should be applied to a restricted range of items. It even suggested that a panel of independent experts should be set up, made of "econometricians, statisticians, experts in indices, marketing specialists and possibly product engineers", who would have to be given training. This panel would provide guidance on conceptual and application issues pertaining to hedonic methods (op. cit., p. 7).

3.2 *Interpretations of Quality*

For his part, François Eymard-Duvernay notes that "the existence of objectivised definitions of quality that remain stable over time leads to the development of intermediaries, operating externally to the contracting parties, whose role will be to verify the soundness of the transactions. Whereas mediation through the market is based on examination of the intentions enshrined in contracts, the definition of standardised qualities opens up the possibility of validating product quality on the basis of data external to contracts" (1989, p. 336). However, third parties also have a part to play in setting forth the exogenous quality criteria, giving rise to the classification hypothesis. Thus Lequiller (1997) points out in passing that "the company AC Nielsen France has been eager to make available to INSEE extremely detailed data on certain markets as part of a joint research programme that begins in 1997", which was to give that international marketing agency very considerable power over valuations. By the end of the 2010s, moreover, these marketing organisations were playing an even greater role in the production of statistics (see Chap. 5).

The Boskin Commission considered it obvious that "consumers of 30 years ago would probably have been willing to pay a price 20% higher to have the privilege of choosing from the variety of fruits and vegetables available to them today in winter compared with those that were available in winter 30 years ago" (Lequiller 1997, p. 17). Beside the fact that this 'obviousness' does not take account of the intrinsic quality of the products, since it is simply the greater variety of produce available in all seasons that in itself constitutes an increase in quality, are there grounds for questioning the environmentally acceptability of this criterion for an increase in quality?

The use of econometric methods is often presented as the objectified solution to the treatment of quality in prices. Even though Griliches conceded that the line separating 'changes in consumers' taste' from 'improvements in quality' was difficult to establish permanently over time, this econometric method met with considerable success among American statisticians in the 1960s and 1970s and was considered a very promising solution to the problem of measuring quality. This craze had its origins in the fact that the hedonic method is, as we have seen, consistent with the standard theory that refers back explicitly to the work of K. Lancaster (1975) and is based on the revelation of price through the market, even in the case of non-market assets, such as the environmental aspects of housing. Many economists attribute to it the eternal promise of intellectual progress.

3.3 *Hedonic Prices: Between Communicative Power and Weakness in Application?*

Is there a suggestion of a myth surrounding the expansion of the hedonic method as a means of capturing quality effects? Over and above the theoretical critiques of which it has been the target, contradictory statements have been made about the expansion of the method.

3.3.1 *Some Theoretical Critiques*

After a period in which the hedonic method was very much in favour, it became the target of increasingly frequent criticism. Some far-sighted appraisals appeared as early as the 1990s, with Piriou proposing a critical analysis of the hedonic method, which assumes that the relationship between price and characteristic remains stable (Piriou 1992, p. 58). According to Piriou, however, the actual instability of that relationship "means that determination of a product's fictitious base price is more problematic than INSEE seems willing to admit" (p. 59). For example, the decomposition of the characteristics of mobile telephony carried out in 2003 (Magnien 2003), which emphasises supply-side criteria such as the number of minutes of talk-time, of calls to landlines, of calls to the same or rival networks and so on, seems out of date 15 years on. Similarly, if an improvement in quality is to have the meaning that the theory attributes to it, comparisons of utilities across time periods would have to be possible. Other authors have challenged the method's effectiveness on the basis of the hypotheses underlying it. One such critic is Bart Hobijn (2002), who demonstrates the need for perfectly competitive markets if the hedonic method is to work. Hobijn shows, in an internal critique, that this hypothesis is never realised in practice, which leads to overestimation of the discount applied to the price because the quality effect is itself overestimated.

3.3.2 *The Hedonic Method's Sphere of Application Remains Narrow*

According to Moulton in 2001, the method hedonic was applied to the prices of 18% of American consumer expenditure (Moulton 2001). In 2006, Hartwig, who considers the discount applied to the apparent change in the nominal index that results from application of the hedonic method to be inappropriate, nevertheless recognised that the "BLS uses it for portable computers, television sets, DVD players, cameras, refrigerators, microwave ovens, washing machines, tumble driers and photocopiers, as well as textbooks and the price of non-residential buildings" (Hartwig 2006, p. 549). The method is not used to any great extent in France: "Because of its complexity, the hedonic price method is, as Moati and Rochefort make clear, applied only to a small number of goods: household electrical appliances (so-called 'white goods'), certain 'brown' products, cars and certain 'fees'. INSEE has stopped applying the method to microcomputers because of the difficulty of dealing with the integration of software packages into the machines that are sold" (op. cit., p. 76). The method is still used for the rent index.

3.3.3 "Consumption Profile" Methods

Long considered the most promising method for estimating quality, use of the hedonic method has ultimately remained limited to a small number of mainly durable goods. A diverse range of methods are used to measure quality today, depending on the goods or services under consideration. Mobile telephony, which is characterised by constant changes in its characteristics (permanent innovation) and a service offer that is highly variable in composition, is ill suited to hedonic methods. INSEE prefers an ad hoc method based on tracking of consumption profiles. It is no longer a matter of tracking a good whose quality remains stable over time but rather of tracking various typical consumers or consumption profiles, which are used to estimate the price that minimises expenditure (Magnien 2003, p. 6). The main underlying, and strong, hypothesis here is that all consumers migrate each month to the optimal product (op. cit., p. 24). This approach is similar to constant utility indices and, "being easier to implement" (op. cit., p. 6), tracks the structure of the constant utility cost of living indices that are presented in the next chapter.

4 Conclusion. Taking Account of Sustainability, the Environment and Care Work

The methods used to treat quality take little if any account of some of the characteristics of goods and services.

This is the case with the sustainability characteristics of goods, and more generally with the negative externalities produced by those goods and services. With regard to agricultural and agro-food products, for example, the spectacular productivity gains recorded from the 1950s through to the 1980s were achieved to the detriment of certain aspects relating to taste and nutritional value or even health, since agrochemicals were used on a massive scale in their production. Similarly, in manufacturing, producer strategies based on built-in obsolescence—which are regularly disseminated in the media—are conspicuous by their absence from product specification catalogues, as is the decline in the sustainability of certain goods. From the producer's point of view, of course, this is quite understandable. If these practices were objectivised and a less promethean vision of the evolution of production and consumption practices were adopted, more nuanced and undoubtedly more complex statements could be made. It would also be helpful to focus less on technology. The excessive technophilia displayed by INSEE statisticians, which can be regarded as a form of social determinism, is evidently linked to the training of the elites in official statistics, most of whom are alumni of France's elite engineering schools, and particularly the Ecole Polytechnique. The question of well-being considered from the point of view of care is not tackled at all in these treatments. Services with a high relational element elude modelling and any attempt to take account of their evolution in official statistics. Similarly, efforts to adopt a constant quality approach to home help services, health services, education or support services face formidable challenges and remain a largely unresolved issue.

References

Aghion, Ph., A. Bergeaud, T. Boppart, P. Klenow, and H. Li. 2017. *Missing Growth from Creative Destruction*. Federal Reserve Bank of San Francisco, Working Paper Series, January.

Baker, D., ed. 1998. *Getting Prices Right. The Debate over the Consumer Price Index*. Economic Policy Institute, London and New York: Routledge.

Boskin, M.J., E. Dulberger, R. Gordon, Z. Griliches, and D. Jorgenson. 1996. *Toward a More Accurate Measure of the Cost of Living*. Final Report to the Senate Finance Committee, December 4.

Delpla, J. 2008. Commentaire. In *Mesurer le pouvoir d'achat*, ed. Ph. Moati and R. Rochefort, 163–168. Paris: La Documentation française.

Demade, J. 2018. *Produire un fait scientifique : Beveridge et le Comité international d'histoire des prix*. Paris: Éditions de la Sorbonne.

Eurostat. 2001. *Recueil de documents de référence sur l'IPCH*. 2/2001/B/5, Luxembourg.

Eymard-Duvernay, F. 1989. Conventions de qualité et formes de coordination. *Revue économique* 40 (2): 329–360.

Gadrey, J. 1996. *Services : la productivité en question*. Paris: Desclée de Brouwer.

Glaude, M. 1997. Du bon usage des indices de prix à la consommation. *Revue française du marketing* 161: 5–20.

Goodman, A.C. 1998. Andrew Court and the Invention of Hedonic Price Analysis. *Journal of Urban Economics* 44: 291–298.

Hartwig, J. 2006. On Spurious Differences in Growth Performance and on the Misuse of National Accounts Data for Governance Purposes. *Review of International Political Economy* 13 (4): 534–558.

Hobijn, B. 2002. *On Both Sides of the Quality Bias in Price Indexes*. Staff Reports 157, Federal Reserve Bank of New York.

ILO, IMF, OECD, the European Communities, United Nations, Eurostat, The World Bank. 2004. *Consumer Price Index Manual. Theory and Practice.* Geneva: ILO.

Jany-Catrice, F. 2018. Conflicts in the Calculation and Use of the Price Index—The Case of France. *Cambridge Journal of Economics* 42 (4): 963–986.

Kokoski, M. 1993. Quality Adjustment of Prices Indexes. *Monthly Labor Review* 116: 34–46.

Lancaster, K. 1975. Socially Optimal Product Differentiation. *American Economic Review* 65: 567–585.

Lequiller, F. 1997. L'indice des prix à la consommation surestime-t-il l'inflation? *Économie et Statistique* 303 (mars): 3–32.

Magnien, F. 2003. Mesurer l'évolution des prix des services de téléphonie mobile. *Economie et statistique* 362 (juillet): 3–31.

Moati, Ph., and R. Rochefort. 2008. *Mesurer le pouvoir d'achat, Rapport pour le CAE.* Paris: La Documentation française.

Moulton, B. 2001. *The Expanding Role of Hedonic Methods in the Official Statistics of the United States.* Bureau of Economic Analysis, June.

Moulton, B., and K.E. Moses. 1997. Addressing the Quality Change Issue in the Consumer Price Index. *Brookings Papers on Economic Activity* 1: 305–349.

Petit, G. 1991. Un nouveau suivi des prix des actes médicaux. In *Courrier des statistiques*, 41–48. Paris: Insee.

Piriou, J.-P. 1992. *L'indice des prix.* 2e rééd. Paris: La Découverte, coll. "Repères".

Schultze, C., and C. Mackie, eds. 2002. *At What Price?* Washington, DC: National Academy Press.

Stapleford, Th.A. 2009. *The Cost of Living in America. A Political History of Economic Statistics 1880–2000.* Cambridge: Cambridge University Press.

Théret, B. 2010. L'argent public et les régimes économiques de l'ordre politique. Entretien avec Bruno Théret. Vincent Gayon et Benjamin Lemoine, 2010/3. *Genèses*, pp. 136–152.

Triplett, J. 1997. Measuring Consumption: The Post-1973 Slowdown and the Research Issues. *Federal Reserve Bank of St Louis Review* 79 (3): 9–42.

Wahl, R.W. 1982. Is the Consumer Price Index a Fair Measure of Inflation? *Journal of Policy Analysis and Management* 1 (4): 496–511.

Waugh, F.V. 1929. *Quality as a Determinant of Vegetable Prices; a Statistical Study of Quality Factors Influencing Vegetable Prices in the Boston Wholesale Market.* Studies in History, Economics and Public Law, ed. The Faculty of Political Science of Columbia University. No. 312.

CHAPTER 5

From Consumer Prices to the 'Cost of Living'

In its public communications, INSEE distances the CPI from a cost of living index, stating very explicitly on its website that: "It must be remembered that the consumer price index is not a cost of living index. The purpose of the consumer price index, after all, is to measure the effects of variations in price on the cost of purchasing products consumed by households. The cost of living index seeks to measure the variations in the expenditure required to maintain households' standard of living at a specified level". Nevertheless, it would seem that most of the methodological changes introduced since the 1950s in both France and the USA have gradually led the price index to move closer towards a *certain* type of cost of living index, or towards an index of the cost of maintaining a *certain* lifestyle (see also Box 2.3).

1 A Hundred Years of Convergence Towards a *Cost of Living Index*?

This convergence is the product of several dynamics. Firstly, the prices made visible by the index have become increasingly complex and consequently more and more difficult to capture in a fixed-basket index. Secondly, the context, notably the succession of economic, social, and health crises challenges the macroeconomic statistics. Thirdly, the shifts in the dominant intellectual paradigm throughout the twentieth century

F. Jany-Catrice, *A Political Economy of the Measurement of Inflation*,
https://doi.org/10.1007/978-3-030-59940-9_5

have led to the acceptance of utilitarianism and, concomitantly, the development of indices that official statistics offices have sought to implement.

1.1 Realities Elude Statistics

The 'observed' realities that have to be reported statistically are some distance removed from the methodological and theoretical ideal. They may even seem to elude the statistics altogether: the mass production of standardised goods distributed through clearly identified channels has been replaced by less uniform production practices whose output is distributed through more diffuse, less easily predictable channels. The mass production of standardised goods has given way to a new form of consumption made up of experience goods, the quality of which is experienced once only after the good has been acquired, of goods with a high relational or informational content or of complex services (education, healthcare, etc.). In his contribution to the debate on secular stagnation, which refers to a condition of no or only negligible growth in a market-based economy, Mokyr (2014) suggests, with regard to informational goods, although the proposal could equally be extended to services with a high relational content, that "economists are trained to analyse macroeconomic statistics, such as per capita GDP and its derivatives, such as factor productivity. These measures were designed for an economy that produced steel and wheat, not for an economy in which information and data are the most dynamic sector" (p. 88).

These changes have been numerous and since the 1960s have been piling up as so many challenges to the price index. They have arisen from the expansion of the service sector in developed economies, on both the production and consumption sides (Griliches 1992; Gadrey 1996; Triplett and Bosworth 2004). The specific nature of service activities, which accounted for 48% of expenditure in the CPI in 2016, seriously complicates price measuring exercises, in particular because in service activities more than elsewhere the very idea of a standard product unit, the basis for price tracking, is very often lacking. One of the characteristics of services is a certain degree of elusiveness when it comes to determining what is produced; there is sometimes also a degree of confusion between output and outcome. The uncertainties of the exchange process and the obstacles to codification and standardisation are all factors that require conventions that break with the traditional Laspeyrian principles of price measurement, as is the case with the measurement of mobile telephony prices (cf. Chap.

4). The development of digitalisation, the resultant expansion of the offer to consumers (in terms of the offer of Internet content, music, films, etc.), the 'free' services that are sometimes associated with it and, more generally, the enormous choice of products and services available in the market are all changes in production and consumption practices that pose formidable challenges for price statistics. The expansion of e-commerce and the proliferation of yield management policies (price policies finely adjusted to consumer behaviour) have made prices very or even extremely volatile, particularly at intervals that are hardly taken into account in the statistics, if at all (e.g. infra-day price movements). The development of the circular economy (sometimes regarded as a new industrial revolution) or what is sometimes known as the 'free economy' (in which purchase prices are undoubtedly zero but production costs and use are certainly not) are all challenges for statisticians, even though the conceptual, theoretical and practical issues are still the object of intense debates, as shown in earlier chapters.

The crises also succeed one another quickly and the Offices of national statistics have to face new challenges, as for instance the COVID-19 crisis has dramatically shown. During this specific crisis, the measurement of inflation has been challenged due to spectacular modifications in the consumption behaviours. In France for instance, the crisis has led INSEE to calculate 'an alternative price index', a Paasche index that would, according to the Institute, better express the price evolution. Indeed, during the containment period, the consumer's budgetary coefficients have dramatically changed: a greater share of expenses dedicated to food, and a smaller share to transportation, and energy. Over a year (from April 2019 to April 2020), INSEE suggests that the use of a Paasche index using the budgetary coefficients of April 2020 leads to an inflation rate of 1.6%. The use of the traditional Laspeyres PCI leads to an inflation rate of 0.3% over the same period.

These changes, some of them far-reaching, in both prices policies and ways of producing and consuming, are all symptoms of a "reality that is disintegrating", to borrow the splendid phrase coined by Boltanski and Esquerré (2016), which make the use of macroeconomic indicators as they were conceived, for the most part, at the beginning of the twentieth century increasingly complex and fraught. The choices made in taking account of these changes provide an opportunity to make visible the innovations—or sometimes the contortions—introduced into the official statistical apparatus in order to deal with them.

1.2 The Intellectual Paradigm

As is implicit throughout this book, the role and place of ideas, and particularly those emerging from the discipline of economics, in the changes in ways of thinking and behaviours (Jasanoff 2004; Orléan 2014) have been decisive. As we have seen, the circulation of ideas in the 1950s was weak, particularly between the USA and France. In the 1990s, the international circulation of ideas was fostered by certain key figures such as François Lequiller, who played a role in arguing for the import of ideas from the world of US economics. The 2000s were marked by the construction of a more homogeneous epistemological community, thanks in particular to two groups of experts: the Ottowa Group set up in 1994 by the UN Statistical Commission, whose strength, it declares on its website, is based "on its professional authority, independence, and usefulness to national and international statistical agencies", and the Eurostat Working Group on the HICP, its alter ego for the EU. In addition to these groups, there are the joint meetings between ILO and the UN Economic Commission for Europe (UNECE). The gradual domination of these groups by mainstream economists—simply reflecting their domination in the academic world—was behind the reforms that were gradually introduced, initially through the changeover from fixed-basket price indices (what the American call the cost of goods index or COGI) to cost of living indices (COLIs), and then to constant-utility indices (CUIs). To give a fuller idea of these trends presented here in broad outline, it should be remembered (see Chap. 2) that historically it was the trade unions that first called for prices indices to be cost of living indices, although they had a very different understanding of the concept of cost of living.

The plan to turn the price index into a cost of living index and then into an index of well-being, which mainstream economists have interpreted unequivocally as a constant-utility index, has been on the drawing board since the 1950s in the USA and is now widely accepted by the statistics profession, at least in the USA (Hartwig 2006; Stapleford 2009). In France, reservations persist, even though part of the profession has been preparing the ground for reforms in that direction. The reasons for these reforms have been shown throughout this book: (i) the increasing complexity of production and consumption practices, which make it impossible to construct strict Laspeyrian indices, as Mokyr rightly suggests (op. cit.); (ii) the alignment of the price index and neoclassical theory, which now dominate the cognitive domain of economic statisticians. The theoretical framework underpinning the cost of living index is based explicitly on consumer theory (iii). A fourth reason has been put forward, which will be examined at greater length in the second part of this chapter. The argument is that COLIs generally trend lower than GOGIs and ultimately function as a genuine devaluating tool. This is what an increasing number of commentators in the world of political economy have argued (Stapleford 2009).

1.3 *A Big Comeback for Utility?*

The main reason for the statistical treatment of quality is the fact that, in Laspeyrian price indices, a fixed basket of goods of constant quality has to be used. Although the idea of constant utility goes back to Konus (1924), it was long confined within narrow circles. In his 1992 book on the price index, which was otherwise comprehensive, Piriou, for example, makes no mention of it at all. The notion of "equal utility" for consumers is found in Lequiller (1997, p. 12), but as the author himself acknowledges, "this notion, which is already difficult to define in the case of one consumer, is even more so for millions of consumers" (op. cit.).

1.3.1 Defining the COLI

On the face of it, an index measuring the evolution of the cost of living can be defined in various ways, particularly because the very idea of 'living' is a difficult and somewhat perplexing one. The definitions generally used to emphasise the monetary aspect of living standards, in which the 'cost' of living is defined as a measure of the variation in the minimum cost of maintaining the same standard of living on the basis of two different consumption structures, one for each of the two periods being compared, and factors other than pure price variations are likely to be taken into account in the index (ILO et al. 2004). However, the definitions that are most consistent with the theories of well-being emphasise the idea that what should be measured is the minimum expenditure required for a consumer to maintain a constant level of well-being, satisfaction or utility (Greenlees and McClelland 2008; Hobijn 2002, p. 3). This type of consideration takes us a very long way away from inflation as a macroeconomic measure of the generalised rise in prices towards the hotly debated question of whether to measure individual or collective well-being (Méda 2008; Gadrey and Jany-Catrice 2016; Stiglitz et al. 2009; Harribey 2013).

1.3.2 Fifty Years After They Were Developed Conceptually, Are Constant-Utility Indices Being Put into Practice?

And yet, since the beginning of the 2000s, there has been a proliferation of studies that have highlighted this concept, which has the virtue of being consistent with utilitarian theory while at the same time parting company with the ambiguity surrounding the notion of quality, opting instead for the concept of consumer utility. The studies by Patrick Sillard and Wilner (2015) are absolutely explicit about the link maintained between constant utility and standard cost of living theory: "This concept (of a constant utility index) is clearly a response to the concern to measure the evolution of the cost of living. Such an index is, after all, supposed to reflect the evolution between two periods of time of the budget a consumer has to devote to her consumer expenditure in order to maintain her utility at the same level as that of the reference or base period" (Sillard and Wilner 2015, p. 759).

The Laspeyres index could then conceivably be replaced by a utilities index (see Magnien and Pougnard (2000) or O'Neill et al. (2017)) that takes the following form:

$COL_{1/0} = \dfrac{C(p_1, u_0)}{C(p_0, u_0)}$, interpretation of which would give a cost of living index 'COL', which is a ratio that compares the cost of achieving a level of utility at the reference time and at current prices with the cost of achieving the same level of utility at the base prices. Ultimately, the arithmetic form is the same as the Laspeyres index (as set out in Chap. 1), the difference being that quantities now give way to utilities.

Already present in the first critical studies of the price index, CUIs can be seen as a means of eliminating measures based on value judgements made by economists or statisticians. Pareto's ordinal revolution was based on this elimination when it sought to make utility ordinal and incomparable between individuals in order to foster the objectivation of economics, to make it a real science without value judgements made by theoreticians. This innovation of the early twentieth century has been reactivated in the twenty-first century, an indication of the advance of utilitarianism in the world of French official statistics. "A function of utility that rationalises data (also) has to be brought to the fore. In formal terms, this problem can be solved thanks to revealed preference theory" (Magnien and Pougnard 2000).

Constant utility indices have several virtues that lend them credibility in the intellectual paradigm. They put an end to the debate on the convention-based definition of quality, which no longer comes across simply as an interesting concept but is replaced by the notion of consumer utility which, according to its advocates, is an altogether more 'rigorous' concept. Above all, they herald the advent of the cost of living index and bring to an end the reign of the CPI as it was conceived in the 1920s. They also open up the possibility of a collective order that is not based on an explicit collective settlement and contribute towards the consolidation of an autonomous science (Postel 2015). However, this use of mainstream theory as a basis for constructing price indices ignores how actual markets function and in particular fails to take into consideration (a) consumers' lack of knowledge about the new characteristics of goods and their uses, (b) the fact that quality is sometimes (to an extent that is itself debatable and dependent on the definition of it that is adopted) constrained by the market and not necessarily wanted by consumers (see Chap. 4), (c) the subjectivity of the very notion of quality and (d) companies' profit and pricing practices, particularly in innovative segments of the economy, etc.

1.3.3 Checkout Data and the CUI

Statisticians acknowledge that it is empirically difficult to construct a constant utility index (CUI) and that access is required to all price and quantity data. In a (utility-based) cost of living index, the quantities are, after all, no longer exogenous to the measure but vary in accordance with the prices in order to take account of substitution behaviours. These advances in the intellectual paradigm found new support in 'checkout data' and suddenly made it feasible to implement this utility-based and welfarist concept of the 'cost of living', at least as far as price collection in traditional points of sale was concerned (accounting for approximately 50% of the prices collected, but only a small share, estimated at 11% in 2020, of household consumption).

Investment ramped up from the beginning of the 2000s onwards in order to introduce checkout (or scanner) data into the construction of the index. Negotiations conducted with large-scale retailers between 2010 and 2016 paved the way for a major change to the index as it will be described in Chap. 6.

The motivations for gaining this direct access to scanned consumption data from large-scale retailers, collected via barcodes at store checkouts, are various. Empirically, it provides access to huge amounts of price and quantity data (19 to 20 million aggregate data items each month) relating to the products actually purchased by consumers. On the face of it, this mine of information would seem to be richer than the 200,000 items of data collected each month by INSEE investigators from points of sale, that is prior to purchase and consequently relating only to price. According to those advocating the use of such data, it should enable investigators to avoid the numerous interpretations they have to make in order to take account of variations in product quality, the disappearance of products, changes to products and the introduction of new products. For some, this absolute transparency of purchasing behaviour, which is so seductive, bespeaks of a fascination with tracking individuals' every move and bringing order to the world (Ogien 2012).

There may also be more practical reasons underlying this propensity for a major overhaul of the system of measuring inflation, and in particular the fact that INSEE is not exempt from the general review of public policies in France and, in a period of budgetary austerity, remains subject to controls on its expenditure. The thousands of items of price data gathered every month at the various points of sale by INSEE price collectors (many of whom are women) come at a considerable cost. By positioning itself within the space created by these mass data, INSEE is able to cut a figure as an innovator. The scientific, digital approach to calculating price variations offers the public institution an opportunity to safeguard the reputation and legitimacy of its outputs, while at the same time holding out the hope of resolving some at least of the problems posed by the evaluation of product substitution and quality.

Another, more subtle motivation is to make available data in keeping with economic theory. Official statistics even seems to be placing itself at the disposal of economic theory: the Boskin Commission was already recommending the use of these checkout data (Silver and Heravi 2003). Sillard is very explicit on this point of view, explaining that the aim of INSEE's checkout data project is "to get closer to the microeconomic foundations of consumer price indices by using checkout data to construct indices that take account of consumers' possible sensitivity to the relative prices of products. These foundations draw on the concept of the constant utility index" (Sillard 2013). It may be presupposed that the technical tools are being prepared for the construction of an indicator based more on the principle of an ordinalist approach to the cost of living.

2 Is Inflation Over- or Understated?

To ask whether inflation is over- or understated is to admit the possibility that there is a genuine standard or yardstick that it is up to statisticians to measure with the precision of a goldsmith, which of course is a long way from the idea upheld in this book that indicators are socio-political conventions and subject to enormous social influence. Nevertheless, ever since the work of the committee chaired by G. Stigler in the 1950s, it has been suggested that the CPI is overstated when compared to a cost of living index, with all the normative and uncertain elements concealed within this notion of the cost of living to which we have already alluded. Presented in the literature as a biased index, in other words one that falls within the scope of metrology in Desrosières' sense of the term, the CPI is said to suffer from four biases: a product substitution effect, an outlet substitution effect, a quality effect and a new product effect (see Chap. 4).

2.1 *Substitutability in Purchasing Practices*

The idea underlying substitution bias is that consumers direct their purchases towards the goods offered at the lowest prices. According to its critics, the Laspeyres index takes little account of these substitution effects and gives insufficient weight to goods whose prices have risen less sharply. We have shown that, since the Boskin Report, substitution effects have been regarded as a significant source of the bias that leads to the overstatement of inflation, in contrast to a cost of living index which, it is argued, introduces geometric means in place of arithmetic means, at least at the level of the micro-indices (i.e. at the most detailed level of the classification of goods, known as 'varieties'). Nowadays, not only do most countries use geometric means to aggregate the micro-indices, but this method is also strongly recommended in the international handbooks.

Nevertheless, various problems are pointed out in the literature. Prominent among them are the implicit hypotheses about consumer rationality, which are taken to extremes in the use of Jevons index. In the USA, for example, says Baker (1998, p. 98), washing machines and tumble dryers appear under the same item of expenditure in the CPI and there is no reason for the changes in relative prices to have substitutive effects. The same observation can be made of therapeutic drugs, which are not, as a general rule, substitutable. Similarly, Baker (1998, p. 101) suggests, if consumers move from more expensive outlets to hard discounters, for example, they are being forced to do so by the decline in their purchasing power. Under these circumstances, they accept that quality will be lower there. However, while these low-cost outlets exist, the history of large-scale retailing shows that traditional super and hypermarkets react by lowering the quality of certain goods themselves. This reduction in quality should be taken into account and give rise to the idea that inflation is understated.

The whole history of the CPI tends to suggest that the traditional estimates of inflation based on a fixed basket of goods should be marked down. During the 1950s, one could read that inflation was 'perhaps' overestimated; since Boskin, however, this overestimation has been quantified, and although it has been challenged, it provided him with the necessary apparatus for objectivation. Although François Lequiller put a damper on the introduction of this idea into the arcane world of INSEE in the 1990s, undoubtedly in order to defend the Institute's credibility, a whole host of studies subsequently combined to suggest inflation was overstated relative to a cost of living benchmark, the benchmark itself not being discussed. Chapter 7 will fully be dedicated to this issue.

2.2 A New Kind of Challenge

In the 1970s, the challenges to measures of inflation which, in claiming to be moving towards a cost of living index, dragged inflation downwards, to the detriment of workers' purchasing power, came mainly from the trade unions, who saw in these statistical struggles a battle for a better distribution of earnings (see Chap. 2). Today, the contradictory assessments produced across the world are no longer the work of the trade unions but of other types of actors, who belong to the world of 'statactivism' and who contest statistics by producing alternative data (Bruno et al. 2014). John Williams, for example, maintains a website entitled 'ShadowStats', which has attracted considerable attention in the USA (Fioramonti 2014), notably because it suggests that, without the methodological reforms, the American index would have increased significantly more than indicated by the official indices.

The alternative data received sufficient media coverage in the USA for statisticians from the Bureau of Labor Statistics, including the director of the prices division himself, to launch a counter-attack. In a lengthy article published in the *Monthly Labor Review*, Greenlees and McClelland (2008) critique in no uncertain terms the idea that inflation might possibly be understated as a result of the various reforms introduced in the USA since the CPI was first designed. They even describe some of these alternative estimations and critiques, which have been "repeated by numerous bloggers and commentators", as "urban myths" (Greenlees and McClelland 2008, p. 6). The defence advanced by the BLS statisticians takes several forms. They emphasise the broad "academic consensus" around cost of living and constant utility theories; they put forward arguments about "consistency" with "international standards" and "statistics manuals", and others about the robustness and rigour of the hedonic pricing method. Stigler's status as a Noble prize laureate further bolstered up this argument.

It is difficult to give full credibility to these counterfactual statistics. What would have happened if the US price index had not undergone the reforms in question, in particular the changeover to the chain index, the introduction of geometric means into the micro-indices and the application of discounts in order to take account of the evolution of product quality? Part of its validity can be assessed by examining the British case.

From 1997 onwards, as a direct result of the Boskin Report (O'Neill et al. 2017), the UK introduced a CPI as a supplement to its retail price index (RPI). This new index generally rises less quickly than the RPI, as the following graph shows for the period from 2010 to 2017. The Bank of England has been using this CPI as the target index for inflation since 2003. The differences between the CPI and the RPI lie in the scope of the two indices (the CPI excludes housing costs and interest payments) and in the method of calculation. The CPI adopts the convention of using geometric means for the micro-indices, with substitute purchases being suggested when the relative prices of the goods change (Fig. 5.1).

The CPI has been used since 2012 as the benchmark for indexing pensions and some welfare benefits. One English website suggests that, on the other hand, the interest rates applied to student loans, which are adjusted for inflation, are still indexed to the RPI. More recently, the British Office for National Statistics commissioned a report from the economist and tax expert Paul Johnson. This Johnson Review is sometimes referred to as the "British Boskin". Indeed, it aims at providing arguments for moving from a Laspeyres fixed-basket price index to a cost-of-living index (O'Neill et al. 2017, p. 266). This report constitutes an outright attack on the RPI which, according to Johnson, should finally be consigned to the history books (O'Neill et al. 2017).

* * *

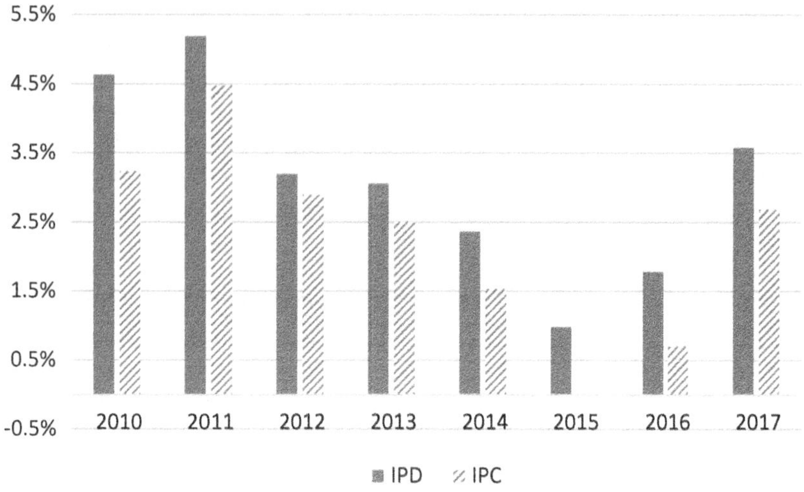

Fig. 5.1 Consumer price index *vs.* retail price index in the UK: 2010–2017. (Source: Based on data from the Office for National Statistics)

All in all, the office of national statistics makes reforms and develops new methods, and lead to a measurement of inflation which is closer to cost of living indexes as expressed in the neoclassical literature (see Chap. 7).

References

Baker, D., ed. 1998. *Getting Prices Right. The Debate over the Consumer Price Index*. Economic Policy Institute, London and New York: Routledge.

Boltanski, L., and A. Esquerré. 2016. L'énigmatique réalité des prix. *Sociologie* 71: 41–58.

Bruno, I., E. Didier, and J. Previeux. 2014. *Statactivisme. Comment lutter avec des nombres*. Paris: La Découverte, coll. Zones.

Fioramonti, L. 2014. *How Numbers Rule the World. The Use and Abuse of Statistics in Global Politics*. London: Zed Books.

Gadrey, J. 1996. *Services : la productivité en question*. Paris: Desclée de Brouwer.

Gadrey, J., and F. Jany-Catrice. 2016. *Les nouveaux indicateurs de richesse* (4e rééd.). La Découverte, coll. « Repères ».

Greenlees, J., and R. McClelland. 2008. Addressing Misconceptions about the Consumer Price Index. *Monthly Labour Review*, August, pp. 1–19.

Griliches, Z. 1992. *Output Measurement in the Service Sectors.* University of Chicago Press.

Harribey, J.-M. 2013. *La richesse, la valeur et l'inestimable : fondements d'une critique socio-écologique de l'économie capitaliste.* Paris: éd. Les liens qui libèrent.

Hartwig, J. 2006. On Spurious Differences in Growth Performance and on the Misuse of National Accounts Data for Governance Purposes. *Review of International Political Economy* 13 (4): 534–558.

Hobijn, B. 2002. On Both Sides of the Quality Bias in Price Indexes. *Staff Reports 157.* Federal Reserve Bank of New York.

ILO, IMF, OECD, the European Communities, United Nations, Eurostat, The World Bank. 2004. *Consumer Price Index Manual. Theory and Practice.* Geneva: ILO.

Jasanoff, S. 2004. *States of Knowledge: The Co-production of Science and Social Order.* London and New York: Routledge.

Konus, A.A. 1924. The Problem of the True Index of the Cost of Living. *Economic Bulletin of Economic Conjecture.* Moscow.

Lequiller, F. 1997. L'indice des prix à la consommation surestime-t-il l'inflation? *Économie et Statistique*, n° 303, mars: 3–32.

Magnien, F., and J. Pougnard. 2000. Les indices à utilité constante : une référence pour mesurer l'évolution des prix. *Économie et Statistique*, n° 335: 81–94.

Méda, D. 2008. *Au-delà du PIB. Pour une autre mesure de la richesse.* Paris: Flammarion, coll. « Champs Actuel ».

Mokyr, J. 2014. Secular Stagnation? Not in Your Life. In *Secular Stagnation: Facts, Causes, and Cure*, ed. C. Teulings and R. Baldwin. London: Centre for Economic Policy Research Press, A VoxEu.org Book.

O'Neill, R., J. Ralph, and P. Smith. 2017. *Inflation. History and Measurement.* Palgrave Macmillan.

Ogien, A. 2012. *Désacraliser le chiffre dans l'évaluation du Service Public.* Paris: Éditions Quae.

Orléan, A. 2014. *The Empire of Value: A New Foundations for Economics.* The MIT Press

Postel, N. 2015. Une approche institutionnaliste de la régulation du capitalisme. mémoire d'habilitation à diriger des recherches, université Lille, décembre.

Sillard, P. 2013. Les données de caisse : vers des indices de prix à la consommation à utilité constante. Document de travail Insee n° F1305.

Sillard, P., and L. Wilner. 2015. Indices de prix à utilité constante et substitutions intermensuelles. *Revue économique* 66 (4): 755–768.

Silver, M., and S. Heravi. 2003. The Measurement of Quality-Adjusted Price Changes. In *Scanner Data and Price Indexes*, ed. Robert C. Feenstra and Matthew D. Shapiro. NBER, University of Chicago Press.

Stapleford Th. A. 2009. *The Cost of Living in America. A Political History of Economic Statistics 1880–2000.* Cambridge: Cambridge University Press.

Stiglitz, J., A. Sen, and J.-P. Fitoussi. 2009. *Commission sur la mesure des performances économiques et du progrès social.* rapport au président de la République. 2 vols. Paris: Odile Jacob.

Triplett, J., and B. Bosworth. 2004. *Productivity in the US Services Sector, New Sources of Economic Growth.* The Brookings Institution.

CHAPTER 6

The Reform of 'Checkout Data'

As we have seen throughout the preceding chapters, measurement of the CPI has been structured by a wide variety of controversies that have punctuated its history and helped to shape it. Inflation is regularly subjected to intense scrutiny and tends to give rise to a certain degree of nervous excitement and tension, regardless of whether the trend is up or down. This febrile state is linked to the redistributive principle underlying the index: as early as 1952, the CPI was being used in France for the automatic indexation of low wages. And even though from the monetarist turning point in 1983 de-indexation policies were introduced, it could be argued that "quasi-indexation" still continues; after all, inflation remains a decisive reference point, directly or indirectly, in wage negotiations and the uprating of welfare benefits, pensions, etc.

The previous chapters also highlighted the considerable social effort required to measure the CPI: this involves recording household consumption in some detail, identifying representative consumers, taking account of cultural changes in consumption, interpreting the degree of constraint in purchasing behaviour, estimating the variation in the quality of goods while at the same time distinguishing it from the introduction of new goods, making innovations in order to facilitate the collection of e-commerce prices and dealing with yield pricing practices. All these activities, which are part of the work of constructing the price index, inevitably rely on a multiplicity of conventions, which are temporarily reflected in methodological choices and then embodied in statistical manuals. These

F. Jany-Catrice, *A Political Economy of the Measurement of Inflation*,
https://doi.org/10.1007/978-3-030-59940-9_6

statistical manuals, and the professionals who compile and use them, have conferred upon them what economists of the *convention* school call an immense "valuation power" (Bessy and Chauvin 2013).

Finally, the preceding chapters also highlighted the great historical transformation of the French price index produced by the succession of small reforms to which the eight generations of indices bear witness.

The purpose of this chapter is to trace the reform of checkout data, with an emphasis on the shift it has produced in the boundaries between the public and private spheres in the process of constructing the CPI. We are not seeking here to argue explicitly that the state is being dismembered or that public data are being commodified. Our argument rather is that the recent changes constitute a modern expression of the reuse of private data by a public actor.

1 Investing in Big Data

As we saw in the previous chapter, the task of rebuilding trust in the price index in France was approached from a number of different angles, most notably through the "checkout data" project. This was a veritable processual revolution, a major technological innovation associated with new price collection practices. This new "regime of digital truth" (Rouvroy and Berns 2013), which marks a radical break with the past, is embodied in a multitude of new automatic modelling systems. When applied to the measurement of inflation, the use of Big Data in official statistics takes a number of different forms.

In some of these forms, the aim is to supplement the price collection process by taking account in particular of new Internet-based commercial practices. This is the case, for example, with *web scraping*, a practice that aims to produce experimental statistics (Blanchet and Givord 2017) in order to fill gaps in the existing data. The aim here is to make use of the contents of Internet sites either in the world of digital technology, mobile telephony and banking or in e-commerce in order to collect the prices of more traditional products. A further aim is to give the price collection process greater legitimacy, since calculating price variations in this scientific, digital way enhances the reputation of and confers a sort of modern legitimacy on the output of the public institution, while at the same time meeting the need for greater control of public expenditure and the size of the public sector workforce.

2 Checkout Data

What we call "checkout data" is one of the forms of Big Data. This project was long in the making. Since the 1980s, when large-scale retailing in France was racked by fierce price competition, consultancy companies have been working in close partnership with hypermarkets. They regularly sell them market research studies on which retailers rely in order to draw up their price strategies and establish their competitive positioning. Thus these consultancy companies collect data for marketing purposes. Through the collection of checkout data, that is the data recorded via bar codes when products are paid for, vast amounts of price and quantity data are garnered and then sold on.

Sparked off by Alan Greenspan and the Boskin Commission report (1996), the lively debate on prices that emerged in the USA in the mid-1990s around the possible overestimation of inflation (see Chap. 4) prompted several major international consultancy companies to contact national statistical offices. In the case of France, one of the consultancy companies made available to INSEE a complete data base on three products (coffee, cooking oil and laundry detergent). The value of checkout data bases is that they provide data not only on prices but also on quantities. Once processed, these data formed the basis of the first study, which was published in 2000. In this study, Magnien and Poulard, two economists working for the French Office of National Statistics attempted to ascertain whether the simultaneous recording of both prices and quantities, made possible by Big Data, could improve the traceability of prices and of their evolution over time. They emphasise the consistency that they say exists between these mass microdata and microeconomic consumer theory, even going so far as to highlight the hyper-rationality of consumers' practices. Thus they declare in their seminal article, which was published in the specialist journal *Economie et Statistique*, that "Calculating a constant-utility index is a tricky affair: it is necessary to identify a utility function that rationalises the data. This problem is resolved formally by revealed preference theory. In practice, very detailed data on prices and quantities are required, which is made possible today by scanner data. This study presents the results obtained with this type of data for mass consumption products: consumer choices, viewed as a whole, are indeed rational" (Magnien and Pougnard 2000, p. 81).

While the question was theoretically and empirically open to debate from the beginning of the 2000s, largely due to these experimental calculations, the project did not really begin to take shape until the end of the decade. The institutional context at that time was favourable, for at least three reasons. Firstly, the period was one in which control of public expenditure was paramount. Now the process of constructing the price index required a workforce of 200 people employed all year round to collect 200,000 prices from 30,000 points of sale in metropolitan France and the overseas *départements*. Secondly, INSEE was facing a virtual loss of its natural monopoly on the production of indices. Various alternative projects were taking shape, along the lines of the Billion Price Project, which is based on Internet data (see Box 6.1 below).

This tendency was part of a more general withdrawal of legitimacy from public services. Finally, other countries had preceded France in using checkout data to calculate their harmonised price index. The Netherlands had been doing so since 2002, Norway since 2005, Switzerland since 2008, Sweden since 2012, Belgium since 2015, Denmark since 2016 and Luxembourg and Poland since 2017. Eurostat appears to have been encouraging the use of these innovations even though at present there is no collective guideline on the processing of this information; not all the countries are working on the basis of, for example, a 'constant concept'.

Box 6.1 The 'Billion Price Project'
The aim of this very large-scale experiment in the USA, conducted by the BPP (Billion Price Project, financed by MIT) and economists including Alberto Cavallo, is to use the vast quantities of price data available on the Internet to produce alternative inflation statistics. One of the advantages of this method, according to its promoters, is that prices can be collected on a daily basis. Although it tries to be close to the official indices, the way in which these new indices are produced sets them apart from the public service; the choices made, the underlying hypotheses and the methods of calculation all reflect new alliances between private web data source (in this instance large-scale retailers) and economists (MIT in this case). There are also considerable methodological differences compared with the methodology currently used in France, in particular the demise of the representative basket of goods and services consumed and the disregarding of quality and substitution effects (see Cavallo 2013).

The French national statistics office developed its project in several stages.

It began by launching negotiations with large-scale retailers from the end of the 2000s onwards with the aim of obtaining access to all their checkout data. Some retailers agreed to negotiate and to test the system, while others were more circumspect. Then from 2012 onwards, INSEE embarked on an experiment with the retailers that had signed up to the project. The aim of the experiment was to process the full-scale checkout data sets made available by the retailers. The project was subsequently to be incorporated into law in the Digital Republic Act, which was passed in October 2016. The retailers were now obliged to hand over these data to INSEE or pay heavy fines, the amounts ranging from 25,000 euros for the first refusal to 50,000 euros for any subsequent refusal.

The price data collected at checkouts are richer in certain ways that are possibly important for statistics. For example, it is no longer just displayed prices that are collected but actual sale prices as well as, and especially, the *quantities sold*, changing the production process from a statistics-driven to a data-driven process (Davis 2017). Furthermore, the richness of the data gave rise to a certain fascination with big data, which came to be regarded as progress because it aimed to be exhaustive (thus in the documents there are frequent references to "six hundred listings for ground coffee", "three hundred listings for pasta", etc.). Thus in the course of an interview conducted for this research, a former INSEE computer analyst told us: "With regard to the checkout data, there's a psychological phenomenon within INSEE, it's a fascination with counts or surveys, the idea that if we could collect all the prices, we'd produce better statistics". However, this very exhaustiveness and the sheer volume of data are not without raising questions of a different order.

3 These Digital Innovations Present a Challenge to the Notion of 'Product'

For the purposes of coordination, economic actors need collective reference points that they share tacitly over a given period. Under certain conditions, statistics can take their place among these reference points, but there has to be agreement on what is to be quantified (Desrosières 2008). When it comes to collecting prices, agreement has to be reached on what constitutes the product and its qualities.

In the traditional price collection system at points of sale, the "product" is defined by criteria recorded by the collectors when the price is collected: a (secret) list of questions is compiled by INSEE and supplied to their price collectors in order to enable them to grasp the idea of "product". To put it another way, from this traditional perspective the power to define and attribute value lies with the public institution that has gradually developed the tools used to categorise and classify. The criteria used to judge the quality of these products are also the fruits of this joint expertise, even though statements concerning them have generally emanated from the world of the producers and the marketers of their products.

With regard to data mining, Rouvroy and Berns (op. cit.) refer in a general way to the idea of "singular cases fragmented by coding". In the specific case of checkout data, the information collected at the checkouts is derived from bar codes or totally unique EANs (European Article Numbering system, the equivalent for Europe of the American Standard Universal Product Code (UPC)). Under certain circumstances, a different bar code may be created, even when from the statistical, economic and consumer's point of view it would appear to be linked to the same "product". The product in question may, for example, be made in two different factories using two bar codes to identify the production sites; different bar codes may also be created for a particular sales promotion, and so on. All this means that official statisticians have had to re-examine the definition of a good or service. Although other countries have decided to take the view that one bar code equates to one good (this is the case in the Netherlands), the basket of goods used by the French official statistical office cannot be a basket of bar codes, which are too unique from the statistical point of view.

Faithful to its statistician tradition, but also because it is committed to working on the basis of a "constant concept", INSEE operates on compromises. Thus it groups bar codes together into what it calls "equivalence classes". These classes are made up of bar codes for products that are regarded as similar from the consumer's point of view.

4 'Exhaustive' but Impoverished Data

In order to create these equivalence classes, access is required to certain product characteristics not available in the bar codes. It is at this point that the market research consultants are called in as reinforcements to obtain this information. These consultancy companies have become a crucial interface between the national statistical office and the outflows of checkout data. In order to obtain the technical specifications that will be used in order to determine product quality and equivalence, product classification systems have long been available and used by these consultancy companies. Thus the production of knowledge is based on these classification systems, combined with the development of new algorithms (there are references to "deterministic" or "alternative algorithms") by teams of INSEE IT specialists and statisticians. The work on developing these new algorithms replaces the empirical analyses carried out by INSEE investigators in the field, whose task it was to interpret the changes, to identify product characteristics, to discover which products had replaced those that had disappeared and so on.

Just as the list of questions used to identify a product used to be put together by INSEE, so the bar codes and characteristics describing goods now tend to be produced by the manufacturers and marketing consultants. These intermediaries' role is not simply to facilitate the flows and transfers of information. They also play a part in ***defining the product quality conventions*** (for both goods and services) that are included in the price composition. They have real power to put a value on quality (Bessy and Chauvin 2013).

This emancipation from subjectification processes is made possible by the "apparent individualisation of statistics" that keeps the "average man" at arm's length through the recourse to "adhesion by default" to the supply of data and through a decline in subjectifying reflexivity (Rouvroy and Berns, op. cit.).

The history of official statistics suggests that the history of the price index is embodied in a series of controversies and crises. Faced with challenges both internal (e.g. changes in consumption habits or in pricing strategies) and external (transition to the euro, injunctions to reduce production costs), the national statistical institute has tried to find compromises between innovative solutions and the importance of guaranteeing the institution's credibility, notably through the stability of its conventions and the beliefs that accompany them. The technological and conceptual innovations are being permanently reworked. They are increasingly clearly aligned with the dominant (economic and neoclassical) theoretical framework, indicating a gradual loss of pluralism. The complexity of the reality undoubtedly calls for a certain epistemological humility, which is most certainly difficult to achieve in the contemporary knowledge regime (see Chap. 7). It is equally clear that the debates around these questions are becoming depoliticised to some extent. This depoliticisation is not unconnected with changes in the composition of the actors involved in these disputes, who themselves reflect a change in society. A former statistician in the French national statistical office told us, "In the forecasting department at the time there were 300 people, 150 of whom were members of left unions. They were the organic intellectuals of the labour movement" (retired statistician). Or again: "At INSEE there were 150 Marxists, no doubt today there's not even one Keynesian left" (former INSEE statistician).

Having previously manifested themselves in disputes between trade unions and official statistics or between trade unions and the political authorities and having once been the embodiment of a genuine power struggle, these challenges are now bringing economists and governments (Argentina, see Cavallo 2013) or economists and official statistics (France) face to face with each other in more discreet forms of conflict and in less blatant forms of power struggle.

The challenge posed by the increasing complexity of social practices has emerged as a serious difficulty for official statistics which, in a fit of pique or for want of resources, have been obliged to toughen and close down its methods and results, to have recourse to new forms of public and private partnerships and to keep citizens at arm's length from these issues, which are nevertheless of general interest.

References

Bessy, C., and P.-M. Chauvin. 2013. The Power of Market Intermediaries: From Information to Valuation Processes. *Valuation Studies* 1: 83–117.

Blanchet, D., and P. Givord. 2017. Données massives, statistique publique et mesure de l'économie. *L'Économie française*, coll. « Insee Références », pp. 59–77.

Boskin, M.J., E. Dulberger, R. Gordon, Z. Griliches, and D. Jorgenson. 1996. *Toward a More Accurate Measure of the Cost of Living*. Final Report to the Senate Finance Committee, December 4.

Cavallo, A. 2013. Online and Official Price Indexes. Measuring Argentina Inflation. *Journal of Monetary Economics* 60 (2, Mar.): 152–165.

Davis, W. 2017. How Statistics Lost Their Power—And Why We Should Fear What Comes Next. *The Guardian*, January 17.

Desrosières, A. 2008. *L'argument statistique*. Tome I: *Pour une sociologie historique de la quantification*. Tome II: *Gouverner par les nombres*. Paris: Éditions des Mines ParisTech, coll. « Sciences sociales ».

Magnien, F., and J. Pougnard. 2000. Les indices à utilité constante: une référence pour mesurer l'évolution des prix. *Économie et Statistique*, n° 335: 81–94.

Rouvroy, A., and T. Berns. 2013. Gouvernementalité algorithmique et perspectives d'émancipation. Le disparate comme condition d'individuation par la relation? *Réseaux*, n° 177: 163–196. Translated by Elizabeth Libbrecht as "Algorithmic governmentality and prospects of emancipation. Disparateness as a condition for individuation through relationships?"

CHAPTER 7

Under- or Overestimation of Inflation?

What are the dynamics that have gradually advanced the shift from a non-committal form of discourse suggesting that inflation might "possibly" be overestimated (G. Stiegler in 1961), to the view, widely held by most mainstream economists in Europe since the mid-2010s, that "the CPI is being overestimated and growth significantly underestimated"? This discourse has gradually turned into a "statement" and has thus taken on the status of a truth that has been naturalised and essentialised. It has repeatedly been taken up by actors who no longer take account of the historical process by which it came into being or of any metadata (used for computational purposes as much as for institutional or political reasons) that might support it.

In order to investigate the dynamics at work in these major changes, we need to draw on analyses of the evolution of statistics policy and the socio-technical conditions of measurement as revealed through the socio-history of quantification (Desrosières 2008; Armatte 2010; Bruno et al. 2016); on the evolution of competition and production regimes (Boyer and Hollingsworth 1997; Boyer 2015); on the evolution of the links between the state and the economy (Boyer 2015; Bourdieu 2012); and on the evolution of the knowledge regime and the space in which representations develop and demonstrate their creative capacity (Fourcade 2009; Jasanoff 2004). In the first part of this final chapter, we will reconsider the importance of the knowledge regime in order to understand why the statement that "inflation is being overestimated" came to be an established truth. We

F. Jany-Catrice, *A Political Economy of the Measurement of Inflation*, https://doi.org/10.1007/978-3-030-59940-9_7

will then return to the history outlined in the preceding chapters, focusing on the controversy around the under or overestimation of inflation. Finally, we will examine the various conditions that came together to pave the way for the statement that "inflation is being overestimated".

1 The Importance of the Knowledge Regime

In according a crucial place to the knowledge regime and taking seriously the social dynamics and power relationships behind the *statements*, our analysis in this final chapter is centred on the discursive production of statements and on the social logics in which these statements are disseminated. Flying in the face of the naturalisation to which they are subjected, this will make it clear that macroeconomic statements, and, among those statements, statistics and indicators, are the result of an intense social effort.

The knowledge regime does not merely serve as a means of ex post justification, used by actors to legitimise a situation, or to conceal interests. Rather, it functions as an interpretation of the reality whose existence it helps to establish. It acts, notably via "discursive coalitions", as suggested by the political scientist M. Hajer (1993), as a medium for the construction of sets of alliances and of coalitions of actors. This act of interpretation not only has a cognitive function that plays a part in constructing the thinking of actors seeking to give meaning to their action but also contributes to the development of a new kind of policy (Baillat 2014).

Economists inevitably play a key role in the knowledge regime, particularly with regard to the statement that "inflation is being overestimated". This role is exercised in a multiplicity of mutually reinforcing ways. Firstly, economists are playing an increasingly central role in the production of official statistics, gradually marginalising the other social sciences (notably sociology) in respect of objects regarded as specifically economic in nature, as is the case with inflation. Secondly, economists are themselves stakeholders in any given society and era (Jasanoff 2004) and cannot evade the hierarchy of theoretical frameworks or the effects of certain socio-political interests. Thirdly, ideas are disseminated through individuals who act as go-betweens, moving from one continent to another: for example, the migration of a body of key economists from Britain to the United States is sometimes said to have triggered the transition from "political economy" to economic analysis and subsequently to economics itself (Boyer 2015). Since then, the profession has been organised on a transnational basis, which has favoured the dominant ideas. Fourthly, the role played by economists is a specific one, due to the privileged connections they maintain with the authorities and hence with the economic policies implemented. Thus Boyer points out that the progress made in economics has influenced public policies; one has only to think of Keynes and the dissemination of his ideas through teaching, albeit with adjustments being made to specific national circumstances. However, economists exploit their symbolic position in the field of ideas in order to "teach the actors to behave like economists" (Boyer 2015), which produces some powerful symbolic effects, sometimes extending as far as a relationship between advances in economics and their dissemination among economic agents themselves.

2 The Dissemination of the Statement that "Inflation Is Being Overestimated"

The socio-history of the price index presented in this volume attributes an important role to the knowledge regime as well as to the major transformations of capitalism. At several places in the book, we have of course highlighted the close link that exists between the price index's redistributive role and the controversies that have punctuated its history. In general terms, after all, if the measurement of inflation is disputed by one social group, for example, because it is thought to be "underestimated", it needs to be understood at the same time that this discourse means that wages too, and indeed all index-linked values also, are being underestimated, requiring public policies to revalue them. Conversely, if another social group (or the same social group at different times) thinks that inflation is being "overestimated", this means, symmetrically, that index-linked values (including minimum welfare benefits, retirement pensions, etc.) are also being overestimated and require "devaluation" policies. The fact that the consumer price index reflects the "preoccupations of daily life", as Braudel (1992) would say, has influenced the feverish tone employed by a wide variety of actors (consumers, economists, industry experts). The entire history of inflation measurement shows clearly that various groups have disputed the truthfulness of the index (both its level and, particularly, its rate of increase), with some suggesting that the index might be underestimated and others that it might be overestimated.

2.1 *First Trade Union Protests Against the Underestimation of Inflation in the 1950s*

The knowledge regime in the years immediately following the Second World War was dominated by Marxist-Keynesian ideas; this had been the case since 1936. The launch of the post-war Marshall plan was to have a lasting impact on the economic policies pursued in France. In the French economic planning system, it was the state's role to be the universal subject of knowledge. This period of large-scale planning conferred a key role on macroeconomics. Graduates of the École Polytechnique placed in the first rank in the competitive entrance exam for INSEE's school for administrators wanted, for the most part, to work in the macroeconomics, economic modelling and forecasting departments. This period also saw the passing of social legislation and regulations that were to lead to the establishment, in France, of a central system of social protection, thanks to pressure from both socialist and communist ministers. In this period of state planning, the state was also the dominant player in the production of statistics. In any case, INSEE was already under the oversight of the Ministry of Economic Affairs. It was against this particular background that the first wage indexation policies began to emerge in France from the beginning of the 1950s onwards. These policies, the aim of which was to maintain or increase employees' purchasing power, also shifted part of the struggle for power away from debates on economic policy towards debates around the measurement of inflation. Thus the indexation mechanism for establishing the level of the minimum wage for 1952, which ensured that the lowest wages maintained their purchasing power, was gradually to shift the focus of protests by social groups against economic policy towards protests against the price index. The government was to intervene regularly to amend the price of the goods in the index basket, thereby implementing the first "numbers-driven policy". The national statistical office was to emerged bruised from this period, traumatised by the manipulations to which its main index, the consumer price index, had been subjected.

2.2 *Second Wave of Trade Union Protest: The Construction of an Alternative Index*

The 1970s were a period of mass production and consumption, standardisation and price competition. This period of mass consumption facilitated price collection, making it possible to envisage real progress being made in the index's arithmetic. The idea that certain consumer products were of enhanced quality led statisticians to experiment with methods that would take account of the evolution of product quality in order to neutralise it, leaving only a 'pure' price index, that is one with all external noise (relating to quantity and quality) stripped out. The years 1970–1980 also saw a sharp increase in the INSEE workforce. Consequently, there was an abundant supply of labour available to gather the price data used in compiling the index, particularly since INSEE was now trying to include more and more goods and services in the basket its figures were based on, and to build an index that would be representative of an 'average consumer'.

However, the knowledge regime was also characterised by the strength of the social power that the trade unions still enjoyed. The social power of the CGT (*Confédération générale du travail*), which was affiliated to the Communist Party, conferred legitimacy on its protests. Arguing that the official price index was "the employers' index" and that it significantly underestimated inflation, the CGT drew up an indicator which, as we have seen *supra* (Chap. 2), was to remain 2 to 4 points above the official index for several years. Quite obviously, this alternative indicator declared, in a quite hostile manner, that the official inflation figure was an underestimation.

This alternative narrative, suggesting that official inflation was being significantly underestimated, emerged at a particular time in history. The INSEE of the 1950s, 1960s and 1970s was also a highly skilled, wealthy, eclectic and pluralist world. By virtue of the reflexive training they received during that era, its statisticians adopted critical attitudes that questioned the various roles of statistics as an instrument of mediation, a shaper of representations and a source of symbolic power. The statisticians, who were accustomed to an interdisciplinary approach, were fully aware that the consumer price index was a "socio-political convention", and that it was the fruit of the power struggles in which some would play a part through their trade union involvement. The aim of this "critical attitude" at that time was not to flush out any possible errors but rather to turn criticism into a "virtue" (Foucault 1990, p. 36) or a code of professional ethics. And, since INSEE's statisticians were strongly unionised at that time, some of them were also using their expertise to assist the CGT in preparing its alternative index, acting in part as trade unionists and in part as professional statisticians. Thus the conditions had indeed been ripe for the production of this alternative indicator.

2.3 *A Counter-attack from the Other Side of the Atlantic: Inflation Overestimated?*

Global capitalism went through a period of radical transformation in the 1980s. There was a sharp decline in standardisation and competition in the developed countries intensified, driven by innovation. The explosive increase in service activities posed some formidable questions for official statistics, both in France and internationally (Triplett and Bosworth 2004; Gadrey 1996), since the macroeconomics indices had been conceived in a world in the midst of industrialisation. At this time, hedonic methods were still considered to be full of promise and, as we have seen, were employed in some of the Boskin Commission's work. Monetarist ideas, which were introduced by Friedman in the 1950s and implemented from the late 1970s in the United States via the monetarist policy of Paul Volker (Chair of the Fed), whose main aim was to achieve a drastic cut in inflation, gradually arrived in France. In 1983/84, economic policies broke with the Keynesian consensus of previous decades and with the Common Programme of 1981, on which socialist president Mitterrand had been elected. Wage de-indexation, competitive disinflation and transnational monetary policies were all introduced in the mid-1980s.

The production of the Boskin Report in the USA was in cognitive harmony with this intellectual dynamic: it was produced with the aim of proving that the price index in the USA at the time was overestimated. Thus the report explicitly states that (p. 3): "Congress and the President must decide whether they wish to continue the widespread substantial overindexing of various federal spending programs and features of the tax code", adding further in the report, "and the increase of the federal deficit and debt". By entering into an alliance with these economists who were arguing for a reform of the index, the US government found a way to exert leverage in order to control public expenditure.

These efforts to cast doubt on the price index played out in a changing institutional and economic context. While the period saw a stagnation in the numbers employed and the labour available at INSEE, its civil servants continued to be highly skilled and its administrators remained in control of the institution's affairs. However, ideas, theories and practices were starting to be imported from abroad, notably as a result of the important role in propagating ideas played by international organisations, such as the IMF, the UN and the OECD, by Eurostat and by senior officials, particularly in central banks.

Although they were contested in France when they were published, the results of the Boskin Report kept alive in the collective subconscious the notion that inflation was "perhaps" overestimated. In the 1990s, the French national statistical office had tried to curb the import of that notion into its arcane world. However, from the end of the 1990s onwards, a multitude of studies combined to declare that inflation was indeed overestimated compared with an (undebated) reference point based on the cost of living. For example, following on from Da Costa (2001) and Hamilton (2001) for the USA and then Beatty and Larsen (2005) for Canada, the statisticians Clerc and Coudin (2010) applied the so-called Engel curve methodology, which had spread rapidly beyond North America. The hypothesis underlying this method is that the share of household budget spent on food is an indicator of well-being regardless of household composition (Accardo 2005). On the basis of family budget survey data, the authors conclude that the official inflation rate in France had overestimated the cost of living by 3% per year between 1974 and 1981. This is a large figure, which would mean that economic growth had been underestimated by more or less the same amount, and then by 1% per year from 1981 to 1994. In the debate that followed publication of the article, an economist sharply criticised the authors' proof, judging it to be in part "tautological" (Gravel 2010). Despite these serious reservations, the narrative around the notion that this time "inflation *is most certainly* overestimated" did become established. Of course this narrative continued to be challenged by various categories of actors, notably the trade unions and some consumers' associations, who tended to see a deterioration in the quality of the goods consumed where experts identified improvements. However, the trade unions, increasingly weakened, and the consumers' associations, regarded as non-experts, were losing the battle of ideas.

3 The Emergence of the Statement that "Inflation Is Being Overestimated"

3.1 The Socio-technical Conditions for the Emergence

Checkout or scanner data constituted a radical technological innovation that permanently transformed the structure of the price index. They provided an opportunity to construct a theoretical framework that was purely microeconomic in character and made use of an empirical base well suited to consolidating the statement that inflation "is" indeed overestimated.

In France, the national statistical office implemented its project in several stages, first launching negotiations with large-scale retailers at the end of the 2000s. Some of these retailers agreed to negotiate and to test the system, while others remained cautious about supplying data to the state. From 2012 onwards, INSEE embarked on a trial with willing retailers. It was supported by Eurostat's publishing in 2017 of a *Practical Guide for Processing Supermarket Scanner Data*, which contains recommendations for the establishment of a system for collecting checkout data. The legal conditions for the introduction of checkout data were also in place in the shape of the 2016 Digital Act, which obliged retailers to transmit these data to INSEE or be fined. What was happening here—and this was nothing new—was that private data were being made available to the public authorities. In return, those companies providing the data were to receive "market benchmark indices as well as data analyses in exchange for the data they provide" (Mehrhoff 2019). As we saw in Chap. 5, the supply of data not only on prices but also on the quantities purchased by consumers enabled the designers of the index to produce something close to a cost of living index (COLI). This "COLI" generalised the recording of substitution effects between products and the close connections with cost of living indices in the sense of the term used in consumer microeconomics, that is constant utility indices.

All things considered, each period of controversy has presented INSEE with an opportunity to try to find solutions to ensure the stability of its conventions and guarantee its credibility. The highly technical nature of the internal debate (Mehrhoff 2019) means that the social actors are excluded, not necessarily deliberately, from a debate that has become restricted to specialists in the field; this contrasts sharply with the period between the 1950s and 1970s, when the trade unions were the main drivers of the debate, which also enabled them to assert their own interests.

Certain similarities can be observed between this increased technicality and the environmental question. Alice Baillat shows, for example, that the proliferation of environmental measures adopted by Western economies in the 1970s was linked to "administrative rationalism", a discourse that puts the emphasis "on the technical nature of environmental issues, which consequently can be dealt with and resolved only by a bureaucratic and scientific elite (Dryzek 1997)" (Baillat 2014).

All these changes meant that the cognitive, political and institutional conditions were now in place to allow widespread acceptance of the statement that "inflation is being overestimated". More and more central banks made the statement their own. The Fed had accepted it since the publication of the Boskin Report in 1996. The Swiss National Bank (SNB) acknowledged that the improvement in the quality of goods and services was not being taken fully into account in calculating the CPI: "measured inflation tends to be slightly higher than it actually is" it stated (see: https://www.bilan.ch/economie/prix_les_chiffres_caches_de_l_inflation). Similarly, the Bank of Canada published an article in 2012 stating that inflation in Canada was overestimated (Sabourin 2012). This statement is also mentioned in reviews of the economic outlook by the private bank Paribas in an *EcoFlash* report dated December 2015, in which it is stated that "this rate conceals an overestimation of inflation of 1% per annum". In an opinion piece in the May 2017 issue of *Bulletin de la Banque de France* (an official publication of the French National Bank), Jean-Luc Tavernier, current Director General of INSEE, also seems to abandon the restraint to which previous DGs had accustomed us: "Many studies", he declares, "have highlighted a problem with the measurement of productivity, with a strong presumption that prices are overestimated and volumes underestimated" (*Bulletin de la Banque de France*, May 2017). As if INSEE were ready for a drastic shift towards a cost of living index, based on the utilitarian framework.

For its part, INSEE seemed absolutely ripe for a drastic change of direction towards a cost of living index based on a purely utilitarian framework which, through the statistical tools it promoted, would tamp down inflation in the sense in which it had been constructed up to that point, since everyone involved in producing the new index now took the "overestimation" of inflation to be an established truth, despite resistance in some quarters (Blanchet et al. 2018). One might wonder whether, within this framework, there were still actors claiming the right, as some did in the 1970s both within INSEE and outside, to examine this truth "for its effects of power, and power for its discourses of truth" (Foucault 1990, p. 37).

3.2 The Pendulum of History: The 'Gilets Jaunes' Effect

In November 2018, a violent social movement swept through the French public space. Known as the "*gilets jaunes*" or "yellow vest movement", it brought together a wide variety of individuals, who tended to be in employment. These workers, many of them low paid, were originally protesting against the introduction of a carbon tax on fuel. Their demands subsequently extended to an increase in purchasing power. In December 2018, the French government introduced emergency economic and social measures in order to increase low wages. Various studies have been carried out in 2019 and 2020 in an attempt to analyse these perceptions of tensions around household purchasing power. Two studies in particular attracted a great deal of attention in the French media.

One of these was a book produced by an economist, Philippe Herlin (2018). Graphically entitled Pouvoir *d'achat. Le Grand mensonge/ Purchasing power. The great lie*, this book deals directly with the *gilets jaunes* movement and aims to 'explain' the gap between their perceptions and INSEE's official figures. To that end, Herlin produced an alternative set of statistics to the official consumer price index. These alternative statistics were based on prices the author had collected over a long period from mail order catalogues. Thus, the author was undertaking an historical reconstitution of prices relative to the evolution of the national minimum wage, with the aim of proving that inflation had been significantly underestimated in official statistics. He focused his proof on various consumer products in the household electrical, clothing, food and motor vehicle categories and on the treatment of housing costs in the consumer price index. At the end of his proof, he concluded that household purchasing power had been declining sharply for 50 years. One year later, another economist, Emmanuel Todd (2020) revisited the controversy. One of the central arguments advanced in the first part of his book, *Les luttes de classe en France au XXIe siècle/Class struggles in France in the 21st century*, is that there has been a general decline in living standards which, he argues, is much more pronounced than the increase in inequalities. For Todd, the general decline in living standards, which INSEE, he argues, does not show, is linked to an underestimation of inflation, which in turn causes the standard of living to be overestimated. The essayist argues that the official inflation statistics are nothing more than 'smoke'. Both authors are advancing the same arguments: they have exhumed controversies that have beset the measurement of inflation for decades, focusing on two factors in particular, namely the quality effect, on the one hand, and, on the other, the share of housing costs in the price index. Both Herlin and Todd dispute in particular the low share of rents in the price index. Since about 40% of households in France are tenants and are the only ones to pay 'rent', which accounts for about 22% of their consumer expenditure, the budgetary coefficient adopted for the price index, at around 8%, is low relative to the 'pressure' that housing costs exert on French households; according to INSEE, it is not the purpose of the CPI to measure this pressure. Both authors are well aware of the fact that economic indicators are based on conventions, which themselves are the product of conflicts and power struggles. By producing such virulent analyses and alternative indicators, both are involving themselves in these power struggles.

They are also contributing to the long history of disputes around the measurement of inflation, which have their origin in the fact that inflation serves a multiplicity of purposes, as an element in the GDP deflator, as a factor in the measurement of household living standards, as a benchmark for the indexation of welfare benefits and as a collective cognitive reference point for wage increases, etc. This new controversy has led INSEE to come out of its shell. A letter from its director general and a detailed critical memorandum pointed out a multiplicity of errors and some conceptual confusions. However, INSEE is embarking on a new project, which will be accompanied from the outset by a blog, accessible to the general public, the first post on which is concerned precisely with inequalities and purchasing power. The French Official Statistical Authority also published a notice in February 2020 that reminded the public of INSEE's independence and the rigour with which its index is produced.

4 Conclusion

What is the outcome of this controversy around the possible over or underestimation of inflation? Over the course of its history, in France and internationally, the price index has seen itself constantly tugged between two sets of interconnected disputes, those around the conventions used to represent wealth (which is what the idea of cost of living expresses), on the one hand, and those around the distribution of wealth, on the other.

This question has been present throughout the 50 years of the index's history and still unsettles communities with different interests. Each one asserts its convictions about what a 'real' price index would look like.

During the 1950s, one could read that inflation was 'perhaps' overestimated; since the Boskin Report, that overestimation has been quantified and, although it has been contested, it laid the foundations for its objectification. Amidst a debate on possible 'secular stagnation', the economist Larry Summers, who notably worked with Greenspan on the fluidification of financial markets, took on board the notion that inflation was being overestimated. In a 2015 lecture on the reasons for the slowdown in productivity in the USA, he advanced the hypothesis that there was "*increasing mismeasurement*" of growth, which he attributed to the underestimation of quality effects. More recently, Philippe Aghion et al. (2017) alluded to "lost growth", blaming the overestimation of inflation; their argument was based on an analysis of checkout databases compiled by the marketing agency A. Nielsen. According to Aghion, this lost growth is linked to the inability of the official statistical system to take account of quality gains in innovative companies. This type of statement, now presented as an obvious fact, is the result of 50 years of struggles to bring it about. The idea is making its way and spreading rapidly in the literature (Groshen et al. 2017; Ahmad and Schreyer 2016) and in the public debate, particularly since Summer and Aghion occupy pivotal positions in the academic 'field'.

Over time, what has quite clearly changed is that the interests of creditors, aided and abetted by a utilitarian economics that has constructed the institutions of its hegemony and the declining power of the trade unions to influence these questions, have now won out over those of wage workers.

Since mainstream economics has claimed for itself the sole right to declare, on the basis of unrealistic hypotheses, what 'living' and its cost are, opposition forces absolutely must be reactivated, including within the official statistical apparatus, in order that competing representations of the convention-based notions that are progress and the cost of living can be debated.

References

Accardo, J. 2005. L'estimation des échelles d'équivalence dans les enquêtes "Budget de famille": les limites de l'exercice. *Séminaire DSDS*, 18 mars.

Aghion, Ph., A. Bergeaud, T. Boppart, P. Klenow, and H. Li. 2017. *Missing Growth from Creative Destruction*. Federal Reserve Bank of San Francisco, Working Paper Series, January.

Ahmad, N., and P. Schreyer. 2016. Are GDP and Productivity Measures up to the Challenges of the Digital Economy? *International Productivity Monitor* 30: 4–27.

Armatte, M. 2010. *La science économique comme ingénierie. Quantification et modélisation*. Paris: Presses des Mines, Mines ParisTech, coll. "Sciences sociales".

Baillat, A. 2014. Pour une approche discursive des politiques publiques environnementales. *CERISCOPE Environnement*, 2014. [Online]. http://ceriscope.sciences-po.fr/environnement/content/part4/pour-une-approche-discursive-des-politiques-publiques-environnementales.

Beatty, T., and E.R. Larsen. 2005. Using Engel Curves to Estimate Bias in the Canadian CPI as a Cost of Living Index. *Canadian Journal of Economics* 38 (2): 482–499.

Blanchet, D., M.-B. Khder, M. Leclair, R. Lee, H. Poncet, and N. Ragache. 2018. La croissance est-elle sous-estimée? In *L'économie française, comptes et dossiers*, 59–79. Paris: Insee.

Bourdieu, P. 2012. *Sur l'Etat. Cours au college de France*, ed. Points Essais.

Boyer, R. 2015. *Économie politique des capitalismes, théorie de la régulation et des crises*. Paris: La Découverte, coll. "Grands Repères".

Boyer, R., and J.-R. Hollingsworth. 1997. *Contemporary Capitalism: The Embeddedness of Institutions*. Cambridge University Press.

Braudel, F. 1992. *Civilization and Capitalism, 15th–18th Century*. University of California Press.

Bruno, I., F. Jany-Catrice, and B. Touchelay (Dir.). 2016. *From Politics of Large Number to Target-Driven Politics. Social Sciences of Quantification*. Springer.

Clerc, M.-E., and E. Coudin. 2010. L'IPC, miroir de l'évolution du coût de la vie en France ? Ce qu'apporte l'analyse des courbes d'Engel. *Direction des études et synthèses économiques. G 2010/04*. Insee, document de travail.

Da Costa, L. 2001. Estimating Real Incomes in the United States from 1988 to 1994: Correcting CPI Bias Using Engel Curves. *Journal of Political Economy* 109: 1288–1310.

Desrosières, A. 2008. *L'argument statistique. Tome I: Pour une sociologie historique de la quantification*, Tome II: Gouverner par les nombres. Paris: Éditions des Mines ParisTech, coll. "Sciences sociales".

Dryzek, J. 1997. *The Politics of the Earth. Environmental Discourses*. Oxford: Oxford University Press.

Foucault, M. 1990. *Les mots et les choses*. Paris: Gallimard.

Fourcade, M. 2009. *Economists and Societies*. Princeton: Princeton University Press.

Gadrey, J. 1996. *Services: la productivité en question*. Paris: Desclée de Brouwer.

Gravel, D. 2010. L'IPC mesure-t-il bien le coût de la vie ? *Économie et Statistique* 433–434: 101–105.

Groshen, E.L., B.C. Moyer, A.M. Aizcorbe, R. Bradley, and D.M. Friedman. 2017. How Government Statistics Adjust for Potential Biases from Quality Change and New Goods in an Age of Digital Technologies: A View from the Trenches. *Journal of Economic Perspectives* 31 (2): 187–210.

Hajer, M. 1993. Discourse Coalitions and the Institutionalisation of Practice. The Case of Acid Rain in Britain. In *The Argumentative Turn in Policy Analysis and Planning*, ed. F. Fisher and J. Forester. Durham and London: Duke University Press.

Hamilton, B.W. 2001. Using Engel's Law to Estimate CPI Bias. *American Economic Review* 91: 619–630.
Herlin, Ph. 2018. *Pouvoir d'achat, le grand mensonge*. Paris: Eyrolles.
Jasanoff, S. 2004. *States of Knowledge: The Co-production of Science and Social Order*. London and New York: Routledge.
Mehrhoff, J. 2019. Introduction. La chaîne de valeur des données de caisse et des données moissonnées sur le Web. *Economie & Statistique*, no. 509.
Sabourin, P. 2012. « Les biais de mesure inhérents à L'indice des prix à La consommation canadien : une mise à jour », Revue de la Banque du Canada été 2012.
Todd, E. 2020. *Les luttes de classe en France au XXIe siècle*. Paris: Seuil.
Triplett, J., and B. Bosworth. 2004. *Productivity in the US Services Sector, New Sources of Economic Growth*. The Brookings Institution.

Conclusion

The purpose of this book has been to open up the black boxes of measurement. In order to analyse the use of statistical data and to give it its full meaning, in both the cognitive (academic research) and practical (public action) spheres, this opening up is a valuable aid to furthering our knowledge. It shows that official macroeconomic statistics, in particular the CPI, as well as gross domestic product, unemployment and debt, are subject to political influence. This influence makes itself felt in the conditions under which the indicators are constructed and in the uses to which they are put. Thus the history of the price index cannot be dissociated from the public policies aimed at improving purchasing power in the post-war years, those intended to increase pensioners' power by raising real interest rates in the 2000s and those aimed at increasing competitiveness by institutionalising wage deflation that we have been experiencing since the 1980s. The two are entangled, interact with each other, set each other in motion, mirror each other and so on.

Far from the direct subordination to a single government that characterised the 1950s or the outright wars between INSEE and the CGT Trade Union in the 1970s, the debates on the official statistics used to measure inflation are now carried on more discreetly, usually between experts, almost all of whom nowadays come from the same epistemic community. The muted debates conducted within INSEE are also marked by intergenerational disjunctions. To oversimplify matters, there are a number of INSEE statisticians and economists, trained in the 1970s, who have

F. Jany-Catrice, *A Political Economy of the Measurement of Inflation*,
https://doi.org/10.1007/978-3-030-59940-9

retained the habit of carrying out structural analyses that emphasise the social relations between groups of classes and regard the political issues around the measure of inflation as obvious facts. This does not prevent them from having the capacity to propose initiatives but they continue to analyse the Institute's output in a very reflexive way. Some of the younger generation, trained in mainstream theory, which they present as being simply beyond question, seek to resolve the issues by adopting a smoothed-out vision of the economy, in which a spontaneous language, that of the market and its pure prices, is regarded as the ultimate arbiter of the truth of individual preferences and well-being.

This relocation of the disputes out of the unions' orbit and into the world of the expert, which regularly burst out of the confines of INSEE, is undeniably linked to the trade unions' weakness and their complete structural withdrawal from the debates on price measurement in favour of engaging with other social issues, notably those connected with working and employment conditions. It is also linked in part to the technical citadels that have been erected between civil society and statistics and its methods, all of which, together with the semantics and the immersion in big data, are all highly technical in nature, and to the drastic erosion of pluralism in the economics profession itself. It is impossible not to perceive the following idea behind these dynamics: the monetarist policies targeting inflation are intended to damp down consumers' expectations of inflation. In order to be able to estimate the rationality of these expectations, the institutions concerned, and particularly the European Central Bank, rely on an index in which the public has complete confidence. As Silver (2006) very explicitly says: "If the public errs in its expectations of inflation, the prices and quantities produced and sold will be affected. The economy will then be functioning inefficiently because the market mechanism will be impaired" (p. 4). Some of the innovative and one-off revisions were clearly intended to quieten down the controversies (a large-scale retail index to placate the Leclerc Hypermarkets; an individualised price index to take the sting out of the issue of the gap between individuals' perceptions and collective aggregates) and to stay on the path of credibility.

INSEE, for its part, is permanently concerned to ensure the institution's strength and soundness by maintaining the stability of its accounting and measuring conventions. Even though the concept of the Laspeyres index based on a fixed basket of goods has long been dented by the proliferation of theoretical and practical innovations introduced since the 1970s (chain-linking, geometric means for the micro-indices, hedonic methods, standard products, checkout data and so on), INSEE's investment in checkout data is an attempt, for the moment, to reach a tricky compromise in the treatment of mass data on the basis of the Laspeyres concept.

The Consequences for Growth and Productivity

The issues we have addressed here are not confined to the CPI but affect all volume-based indicators. Inflation is, after all, an important input in the GDP deflator and acts as a direct indicator of economic growth (evolution of GDP volume), on the one hand, and productivity gains (evolution of the volume of output divided by input), on the other. Thus all the struggles, debates and controversies around the measurement of inflation have a direct effect on these macroeconomic parameters (Jany-Catrice 2018). Most of the economists and experts who assert that official inflation is overstated automatically consider that growth and productivity gains are understated by a proportional amount. Similarly, those who believe that the official statistics obviously understate inflation take the view that growth and productivity gains are overstated. Without directly engaging with this head-to-head debate, which attaches far too much weight—and isn't that a rather delicious paradox?—to the idea that the cost of living could be measured with less bias than a fixed basket of goods, this book emphasises, on the contrary, the constructed component of these macroeconomic indicators and the forces that ensure its legitimation.

* * *

The political economy of the price index reminds us, if such a reminder were necessary, that official statistics are all the result of socio-political compromises and that an immense amount of contradictory interpretations are inevitably at work in the production of statistics. The makeshift measures that are an inherent part of official statistics—and which help objects hold on in a changing world—stand in stark contrast to the naturalised rigour of the macroeconomic outputs of which they are, nevertheless, the direct result. Democracy can only gain from these contradictory interpretations being debated and the compromises objectified; in this way, everyone—economists and citizens alike—will be able to take the part that is rightly theirs in these debates of great public interest.

References

Jany-Catrice, F. 2018. Conflicts in the Calculation and Use of the Price Index—The Case of France. *Cambridge Journal of Economics* 42 (4): 963–986.
Silver, M. 2006. Core Inflation Measures and Statistical Issues in Choosing Among Them. *IMF Working Paper*, April.

Index[1]

[1] Note: Page numbers followed by 'n' refer to notes.

F. Jany-Catrice, *A Political Economy of the Measurement of Inflation*, https://doi.org/10.1007/978-3-030-59940-9

The manufacturer's authorised representative in the EU is Springer Nature Customer Service Centre GmbH, Europaplatz 3, 69115 Heidelberg, Germany. If you have any concerns regarding our products, please contact ProductSafety@springernature.com

Printed and bound by CPI Group (UK) Ltd, Croydon, CR0 4YY
30/09/2026
02225260-0010